Good Morning Children

My First Years in Early Childhood Education

By
Sophia E. Pappas

EasyRead Large

Copyright Page from the Original Book

© 2009 Sophia E. Pappas
Published by Gryphon House, Inc.
PO Box 207, Beltsville, MD 20704
800.638.0928; 301.595.9500; 301.595.0051 (fax)

Visit us on the web at www.gryphonhouse.com

All rights reserved. No part of this publication may be reproduced, stored in a retrieval system, or transmitted in any form or by any means, electronic, mechanical, photocopying, recording or otherwise, without the prior written permission of the publisher. Printed in the United States of America. Every effort has been made to locate copyright and permission information.

Cover Photo: Straight Shots Product Photography, Ellicott City, MD; www.get-it-shot.com.

Library of Congress Cataloging-in-Publication

Pappas, Sophia E.
 Good morning, children : my first years in early childhood education / by Sophia E. Pappas.
   p. cm.
 ISBN 978-0-87659-078-2
 1. Preschool teaching--New Jersey--Newark. 2. Children with social disabilities--Education (Preschool)--New Jersey--Newark. I. Title.
 LB1140.245.N494P37 2009
 372.11--dc22

2008043296

This optimized ReadHowYouWant edition contains the complete, unabridged text of the original publisher's edition. Other aspects of the book may vary from the original edition.

Copyright © 2010 Accessible Publishing Systems PTY, Ltd. ACN 085 119 953

The text in this edition has been formatted and typeset to make reading easier and more enjoyable for ALL kinds of readers. In addition the text has been formatted to the specifications indicated on the title page. The formatting of this edition is the copyright of Accessible Publishing Systems Pty Ltd.

Set in 16 pt. Verdana

ReadHowYouWant partners with publishers to provide books for ALL Kinds of Readers. For more information about Becoming A (RHYW) Registered Reader and to find more titles in your preferred format, visit:
www.readhowyouwant.com

TABLE OF CONTENTS

Dedication	i
A Note from the Author	iii
Preface	viii
Introduction	xv
Part One: Becoming an Effective Teacher: Reflections on My First Year	1
DECEMBER: Teaching Pre-K?	2
JUNE 28: Not a Coddling Mentor	5
JULY: Reflections on Mark and Training at Teach For America's Summer Institute	7
JULY 26: Toward Understanding and Competence	10
NOVEMBER: Still Stumbling—The Process Continues	12
DECEMBER 3: Out of a Rut: Stepping Back to Reflect on Leadership	14
FEBRUARY 27: One Step Closer to Pre-K	15
MARCH 2: Happy Birthday Dr. Seuss and Ms. Pappas: A Pre-K Placement at Last	17
MARCH 9: Ups and Downs: The Journey Continues	20
AUGUST 20: The Wheels on the Bus	22
AUGUST 20: A Classroom of My Own	24
AUGUST 23: Beyond the Paper-Covered Walls: Making Room 111 a Conducive Learning Environment	27
AUGUST 24: Tables and Relationship-Building	29
AUGUST 25: The Teacher's Desk and Leadership	34
AUGUST 25: A First Encounter	36
AUGUST 31: Preparing for the First Week of School	38
SEPTEMBER 4: Planning for the Big Day	41
SEPTEMBER 4: Crafting an Early Childhood-Friendly Schedule and Approach to Families	44
SEPTEMBER 6: The First Day of Class (Classroom Setup Before the Students Arrive)	48
SEPTEMBER 6: The First Day of Class (Classroom Setup Before the Students Arrive—Breakfast)	55

SEPTEMBER 6: Welcome to Pre-K 111	60
SEPTEMBER 6: After the Meet and Greet: Adjusting to a Full Day of School	66
SEPTEMBER 26: My First Observation—Anticipating Mark's Arrival	70
SEPTEMBER 26: My First Observation—After Mark Arrived	75
JUNE 15: No Longer a Novice	81
Part Two: Growth and Goals: Insights from the Classroom and Beyond	**82**
Introduction	83
Becoming Friends and Active Learners: Social Growth in Pre-K	87
DECEMBER 6: Going Above and Beyond	89
DECEMBER 7: Making Peace	91
DECEMBER 16: The Horror of Sharing	98
JANUARY 11: The Making of Problem Solvers	100
JANUARY 15: Reflections on Batman and Madam Speaker	104
JANUARY 20: The Rehabilitation of an Anti-Sharer	108
FEBRUARY 1: Bringing It Off	110
FEBRUARY 2: Forging an Agreement	113
FEBRUARY 6: R-E-S-P-O-N-S-I-B-I-L-I-T-Y	116
FEBRUARY 28: Accidents Happen	118
MARCH 6: Honoring Our Contract	122
APRIL 3: Bad Behavior Solved, Not Made, in High-Quality Pre-K	125
APRIL 24: Peace in Pre-K and Beyond	128
MAY 16: A Listening Ear	131
MAY 24: Coping with the Bad Days	134
MAY 26: Recognizing the Power of Pre-K	137
MAY 30: Saying Goodbye	141
Leadership in a Pre-K Classroom: Setting Goals, Building Relationships, and Managing Effectively	145
DECEMBER 8: Classroom Site Visits	147

DECEMBER 9: Site Visits—Observing Model Early Childhood Classroom Programs	153
DECEMBER 15: Curriculum Connections	158
DECEMBER 18: Taking Charge	162
DECEMBER 20: Creative Thinking, Simple Resources	164
DECEMBER 21: Not Your Grandmother's Scantron: Assessments in a Pre-K Classroom	166
JANUARY 16: Out of Her Shell	170
JANUARY 19: Which Comes First, the Assessment or the Children?	175
FEBRUARY 12: To Teach or to Assess? Is That Really the Question?	178
FEBRUARY 14: The Saving Grace of Effective Transitions	182
FEBRUARY 25: Dealing with the "F" Word	185
MARCH 7: Tackling the Digital Divide	189
MARCH 20: Whose Curriculum Is it Anyway?	192
MARCH 28: Not All Assessments Are Created Equal	198
APRIL 17: Tax Tips: IRS Says I Am Not an Eligible Educator	202
APRIL 19: Praise with a Purpose	203
MAY 3: A Sign of Equality for Pre-K Teachers	207
MAY 21: Snowed Under	208
JUNE 12: The Tough Questions	211
JUNE 13: The Frightening Prospect of Self-Fulfilling Prophesies	215
JUNE 22: A Fair Shot	220
From Good to Great: Academic Growth in Pre-K 114	223
DECEMBER 12: Wow!	225
JANUARY 3: Students as Teachers: An Amazing First Day Back	227
MARCH 22: The Power of Planning	230
MARCH 23: Center Cards and Math/Literacy Enrichment	233
APRIL 27: Awana's Struggles and Successes	236
MAY 1: Ready for Take-Off: David's Story	239

MAY 7: Becoming Social: Karen's Journey into Our Community	243
MAY 10: Center Time=Critical Time for Student Growth	246
JUNE 7: The Pudding	249
Families, Students, and School—Building a Strong Foundation	252
DECEMBER 10: Learning from Each Other	254
JANUARY 9: A New Year: Pre-K 114's Resolutions for 2007	257
JANUARY 21: And Still He Rises...	260
JANUARY 23: Home-School Disconnection	262
FEBRUARY 26: Lessons in Diplomacy	265
MARCH 16: Women Making History in Our Own Lives	268
APRIL 6: The Benefits of Pre-K: A Family Member's Perspective	271
JUNE 19: Summer Learning	274
Epilogue	277
Afterword	281
Appendix	286
General process a teacher can follow to create individualized behavior contracts:	290
Back Cover Material	294

Dedication

To my preschool students:

Give yourselves a kiss on the brain for being such creative and critical thinkers, and give yourselves a humongous hug for acting so kind and responsible. I love you all and feel privileged to have been your teacher. As you move on through elementary and high school, college and beyond, remember what we used to say: "You can do it, I know you can."

***

To my students' families:

Thank you for entrusting me with the care and education of your children in their first year of schooling. Our partnership was crucial to your children's success. I know we share the belief that your children can go "sky high," as one of you once told me; and I hope the foundation we built will facilitate the realization of their potential in the years to come.

***

To my readers:

I hope to spark an ongoing dialogue around the prospects and challenges of high-quality early childhood education with a diverse group of stakeholders, including teachers, administrators, parents and family members, policymakers, the media, and others interested in the topic. Please visit sophiapappas.com to continue the conversation and to email me directly.

***

It is purely coincidental that the title of this Gryphon House book, *Good Morning, Children,* is similar to the website for Good Morning Children, Ltd. There is no direct or implied partnership between the two companies. However, if you are looking for educational resources for young children, you might visit www.goodmorningchildren.com.

A Note from the Author

This memoir and my growth as a teacher would not have been possible without the support of many individuals. First, the Teach For America-Newark staff provided the steadfast guidance and encouragement I needed to become a strong leader for my kids. Susan Asiyanbi, John White, Mark Williams, and Abigail Wentworth challenged me to step up and to believe in myself even when I felt disappointed in my performance those first few months in the classroom. I have to extend a special thanks to Mark Williams in particular, for the countless hours he spent observing my teaching and guiding my self-reflection process. His mix of tough love and high expectations for me and my students strengthened my independent problem-solving skills in the classroom. Secondly, Ms. Morrison, my teaching assistant with years of experience in early childhood education, taught me a great deal about meeting the needs of pre-K students and working with families. Our collaboration throughout the three years I taught at Carter Elementary School produced strong results for our Pre-K 111 and Pre-K 114 students. Moreover, our friendship made each day a pleasure.

Thank you to Libby Doggett, Executive Director of Pre-K Now, for giving me the opportunity to share my experiences and engage others in a dialogue around high-quality pre-K through Pre-K Now's blog, *Inside Pre-K,* during the 2006–7 school year. I also want to thank Mathew Mulkey, Director of Communications at Pre-K Now, for training me on the technical use of the blog and editing my entries on a weekly basis. The blog advanced my own professional development by serving as an outlet for my reflections and as a way to share best practices with other teachers. This book would not have been possible without the blog because Gryphon House publishers contacted me after reading about my experiences on the site. Gryphon House has been such a strong and pivotal partner in the creation of this work. Thank you for taking a chance on a first-time writer and thereby giving a voice to my experiences and the experiences of my students.

My involvement in Teach For America's early childhood education initiative, while I was teaching, also helped me improve my craft and share my insights with other teachers preparing to enter the classroom. Thank you to Alisa Szatrowski for putting ideas and reflections from my classroom in an ECE training text for Teach For America corps members. And thank you to Catherine Brown, former Director of Teach For America's ECE initiative, for giving me the chance to help train Teach For America's first cohort of ECE teachers. Catherine Brown and Lee McGoldrick, Vice President of Growth Strategy at Teach For America, moreover, gave me the opportunity to strengthen my skills as a leader by hiring me to spearhead efforts to bring more of our nation's future leaders into pre-K classrooms in rural and urban regions across the country. I am also grateful to Wendy Kopp, both for inspiring me with her own steadfast leadership in the fight to eliminate educational inequity and for supporting my efforts, first to grow the early childhood education initiative at Teach for America and then to share my classroom insights in this book. Lastly, Teach For America's national ECE advisory board consisting of experts in the early childhood education field provided insight from their years of experience in the field that helped me situate my time in the classroom within the broader context of ECE in our country.

Kathleen O'Pray, the other pre-kindergarten teacher at my school, brought decades of experience, both as a lower-elementary teacher and CBO Director to Carter. I am grateful to her for helping me gain a better understanding of the nuances of our pre-K curriculum, for sharing best practices from her classroom, and for welcoming my ideas. And thank you to Kathleen, John Holland, Abigail Wentworth, Cheryl Steighner, and all others who supported my efforts to generate a dialogue among other early childhood educators by contributing comments to my blog.

Thank you to the other teachers and administrators at my school for welcoming me into the Carter family from day one. In particular, I want to acknowledge my principal for supporting my efforts to build strong relationships with my students and families by allowing me to hold special family events in my classroom such as our "Giving Thanks" party and "Family Show and Tell." Thank you to the cafeteria, custodial, and clerical office staff for providing various forms of support that helped me serve the needs of my students and their families. Also, thank you to my first master teacher from the district for providing constant encouragement and the positive reinforcement that helped give me the confidence I needed that second time around as a teacher.

My family and friends have also been critical to my growth on so many levels. First, my mother and father have always stressed the importance of education. Thanks, Mom, for challenging the school psychologist at my kindergarten screening test to see the true potential behind my shy demeanor. That story continues to help me understand the importance of investing considerable time in getting to know my own students rather than passing judgments based on their behavior the first days and weeks of school. Thanks, Dad for providing me with such a strong example through all your hard work, integrity, and perseverance. And to my siblings, Joey and Christina, thank you for being a constant source of unconditional support and comic relief, especially during those difficult times my first year in the classroom. To Jo-Jo, Vicki, Jeralyn, and Sam, my dear friends from childhood: thanks for always taking the time to listen and taking a strong interest in my class. I must also acknowledge my boyfriend, Greg, who helped me overcome challenges and build on successes by listening to me on the tough days and celebrating with me on the good ones. Thanks to all of my family and friends who shared their diverse experiences with my students either by visiting our classroom or via email: Kopa, Stephanie, Jo-jo, Jeralyn, Justin, Matt, Vicki, Greg, Dad, Mom, Christina, Alicia, John, Alex, Evanthea, and Renata.

I must also acknowledge, once again, my students and their families. Their stories are the heart of this book and the driving force behind my commitment to education reform in our country.

Preface

When I think about the future of our society, its opportunities, power dynamics, and overall vibrancy, I think about my kids—my pre-Kindergarten students—whose needs, strengths, personalities, and families commanded my full attention for three years. Each year, these students entered my classroom at a crucial stage of their development, a period that would help shape much of their mental processes as well as their attitudes towards themselves and others. How I treated them, how I addressed their needs and interacted with their families, would significantly influence their life trajectories. I took these responsibilities seriously and used them to guide my approach to teaching.

> "Keep in mind always the present you are constructing. It should be the future you want." (Walker 1989)

I entered the classroom in 2003 as a Teach For America corps member in Newark, New Jersey. After studying political systems and leaders, both in my undergraduate courses at Georgetown and as an intern on Capitol Hill, I knew I wanted to play an active role in rectifying societal inequities, but I did not know exactly how I could give back to the world. Although I wrote an almost 200-page thesis on education reform in post-apartheid South Africa and U.S. inner cities, I felt removed from the real challenges facing disadvantaged communities and unsure about how to overcome these challenges. Short-term, superficial attempts to address our nation's greatest injustice seemed to haunt the history of education reform; and the persisting gaps between children in low-income and high-income areas mock the very notion of equal opportunity. I sought a solution that reflected the complexity and urgency of the problem. Teach For America proposed a groundbreaking way to address this crucial issue: enlist our nation's most promising future leaders in a movement to ensure that all children, regardless of their circumstances, have the opportunity to receive an excellent education. During my two-year commitment to Teach For America and additional third year in the classroom, I would gain firsthand the insights necessary to effect systemic change while helping my students acquire concrete skills they could take with them to the next grade. That unique combination of impact and learning was critical to my decision to take hold of the opportunity that Teach For America offered: the chance to lead a group of children toward excellence, and to understand more fully the prospects and challenges that come with trying to ensure that our educational and cultural institutions respect and uphold the dignity and worth of all children as individuals. The success I experienced with my students would solidify my belief in the ability of our country to tackle a problem that many deem a lost cause. After seeing my students "beat the odds" at the pre-K level, I can move forward both with the knowledge that breaking down cycles of poverty is possible, and that my teaching experience provided me with a foundation of firsthand insights into how to achieve that goal. Moreover, because I am part of a network of more than 12,000 Teach For America alumni serving in a variety of professional positions, all working to improve the life prospects for students everywhere, I know that I am not alone in this endeavor.

The rigor and intensity of Teach For America's selection process introduced me to an organization intent on giving students in rural and urban low-income areas the high-quality instructional leaders they deserve. In the days after my interview with Teach For America, I remember anxiously awaiting a response, concerned that I did not adequately convey my passion for eliminating educational inequity. I was ecstatic when I received the acceptance letter. Yet at that point, I could not imagine what a profound impact my experience as a Teach For America corps member would have on the way I saw education reform and my future life path.

My students resided in a low-income area in Newark, New Jersey. Most of their life circumstances put them at a greater statistical risk for dropping out of high school, as well as experiencing future incarceration, teenage pregnancy, and unemployment. When they entered school at age four, they were already behind their peers in more affluent communities. Indeed, according to Nobel Laureate of Economics, James Heckman, nearly half of the achievement gap we see in high school between African-American and Caucasian children is already present before kindergarten. Providing high-quality pre-K education to children from low-income areas is one of the first steps in leveling the playing field; it helps close the achievement gap before it widens even further. Such programs are certainly not a panacea, but they are a necessary step in improving the quality of early childhood education. Recent increases in support among policymakers in various states suggest that interest in such programs is growing. In 2007, nearly 30 governors pushed for more funding for their state pre-K initiatives (Vu 2007). Teach For America started strategically placing cohorts of pre-K teachers in some of its regions in 2006 and is likely to reach over 8,000 three-and four-year-olds in 2010.

While these proposals are encouraging, it is important that individuals and organizations move forward with a nuanced understanding of the challenges and prospects facing all pre-K programs. First, policymakers need to maximize the positive impact of their initiatives by shaping and supporting programs with effective educators and sound accountability structures. If districts or states are going to develop criteria for selecting and evaluating pre-K teachers, they need to have a clear picture of the characteristics of effective educators. Likewise, if they are designing assessment systems and curricula, a teacher's perspective on the accuracy and value of different forms of assessment and curricula would be invaluable. Educators, family members, and the media also need an informed opinion as they evaluate these programs. That is why when I heard that the organization Pre-K Now—a national non-profit advocating high-quality, voluntary pre-K for all for all three-and four-year-olds—was looking for a teacher to share her insights through a weekly blog, I thought I could help by contributing my experiences to the debates surrounding early childhood education. I also wanted to engage teachers and others interested in pre-K in discussions on topics ranging from how best to teach letter recognition to the investment of family members in my classroom. I certainly did not (and still do not) have all the answers. Rather, I wanted to use the blog as a way to describe my growth as a teacher and aspiring policymaker. With this in mind, my entries reflected on my daily experiences. I wrote two to three pieces a week, and responded to comments my readers posted. In the process, I gave my students and their families a voice in this country's discourse on how best to serve our youngest and most impressionable learners.

I started the blog by brainstorming possible topics: the structure of our day, students' struggles with basic literacy skills, students with varied levels of family support, and so on. As I moved forward, I realized that the most substantive pieces I wrote came more naturally from listening to and watching my students. If I was going to tell their stories, the subjects of my entries needed to develop from those issues that stood out at any given time, rather than an artificial timeline I created on a Sunday afternoon away from the classroom. In a sense, this process mirrors the way I became an effective pre-K teacher. I started with a scripted curriculum that dictated lessons for my students before I even knew their names. The program, divorced from my students' actual needs and learning styles, could not provide a solid academic and social foundation. The weekly themes and daily scripts could not meet my students where they were, and then get them to where they needed to be. Once I designed long-term plans and daily lessons using student anecdotes and work samples and state standards for pre-K, I started to see progress.

This process, more broadly, speaks to the importance of understanding the situations educators seek to change. My time as a Teach For America corps member taught me that if we want to shape academic opportunities that will close the achievement gap, we must have firsthand insight into the experiences of children at the losing end of those disparities. As a pre-K teacher in an inner-city public school, I was not only on the front lines. I was a leader on the first line of defense against educational inequity.

Vu, Pauline, "Early ed gains Momentum in the States," Stateline.org, 25 June 2007.

Walker, Alice. *The Temple of My Familiar.* New York: Washington Square Press, 1989.

Introduction

This book is a collection of my reflections on my first two years in a pre-K classroom, blog entries from my third year of teaching, and concrete tools for early childhood educators. Most of the details pertaining to students in my class, however, are from the 2006–2007 school year.

It was hard to determine the scope and target audience of this book because my reasons for becoming a teacher and insights that grew from my experiences in the classroom get to the core of so many different facets of my background, worldview, and future aspirations. I could speak to academics and policymakers after studying race, culture, and politics as an undergraduate and then witnessing the successes and shortcomings of education reform efforts firsthand in the classroom. I could address a much broader audience as a deeply proud American whose family achieved incredible social mobility after just two generations in our country, but who views the gap between the promises of our founders and the reality of stark societal inequities. This book could also use my development as a classroom leader as an example of the kind of change my generation as a whole can achieve. I decided, however, to target my story primarily towards educators. Teachers have so much influence in our society, and yet we still struggle to understand fully how teachers become effective, whether or not they come from traditional education backgrounds. I certainly do not have all the answers, but I hope to contribute my experiences to this ongoing dialogue.

Here are a few of the 14 incredible four-year-olds who started school for the first time in my class during that year. All adults' and children's names, including blog entries, have been changed throughout the book to protect their identity.

- Tyrone—or Doctor Smith, as we called him in Dramatic Play—had a strong foundation in basic literacy knowledge, but he was not very invested in the class at the beginning of the year. His attention span was shorter than most of the children during circle time, and he was often sitting and looking around the room, not participating with the other children or listening to me. He showed improvement in this over the course of the school year, and began to respond positively to activities such as singing songs about his classmates, as well as other more hands-on tasks.

- Kevin came to school with strong math and literacy foundations. He picked up new academic concepts quickly and consistently participated in class activities. Socially, however, he struggled and frequently cried when he was not picked for an activity or had to wait his turn. He was the only child in his household, which may account for some of the difficulties.
- Karen arrived in my class with a strong academic foundation, but until coming to school, she did not have much contact with other children. She had been around adults for most of her early years and initially displayed a hesitance to interact with the other children. From day one, she followed directions and was focused and actively engaged in whole-group activities. Over the year, Karen made real progress interacting with the other children, particularly in smaller groups, and frequently read, shared, and played with her classmates.

I was also fortunate to have a teacher's aide, Ms. Morrison, who has been working with young learners for more than 20 years. Her experience was immensely helpful, and our students benefited from our strong collaboration.

I hope this book sheds light on the lives we hoped to enrich through high quality pre-K.

Learning Labs, Centers, and Choice Time: A Note About Terminology

My school used a scripted program my first year in the classroom. At that time, the district allowed each school to choose from several research-based pre-K curricula.

The scripted curriculum focuses on a different theme each week. Children spend about two hours per day in learning labs. The labs are similar to centers in that children choose to play in one of 10 areas. In each, they explore and learn a wide range of skills and concepts. Teachers change some of the materials in the labs each week to correspond to each theme (for example, for the theme "Pet Parade" the teacher would transform the Dramatic Play learning lab into a pet store) and generate enthusiasm for the thematic developments during the lab tour and while they interact with children during the actual lab time.

After my first year in the classroom, the Newark Office of Early Childhood decided to adopt a single curriculum for all of the Abbott pre-K programs in the district (both school and center based). Instead of prescribed weekly themes, teachers develop topic studies with children that can go as long as the children's interest in that topic lasts. Children spend about two hours per day in centers, which are similar to labs, but are called "Choice Time" to emphasize the importance of the child's choice during that time. Teachers build on students' interests to advance their skill and knowledge base by interacting with them during choice time using their knowledge of each child's strengths and weaknesses.

Note: At times in the classroom, I deviated slightly from both curricula to meet the needs of my students. For purposes of clarity, in this book I will use the terms for the scripted curriculum when talking about my first year and those for the other curriculum when talking about subsequent years in the classroom.

Part One

Becoming an Effective Teacher: Reflections on My First Year

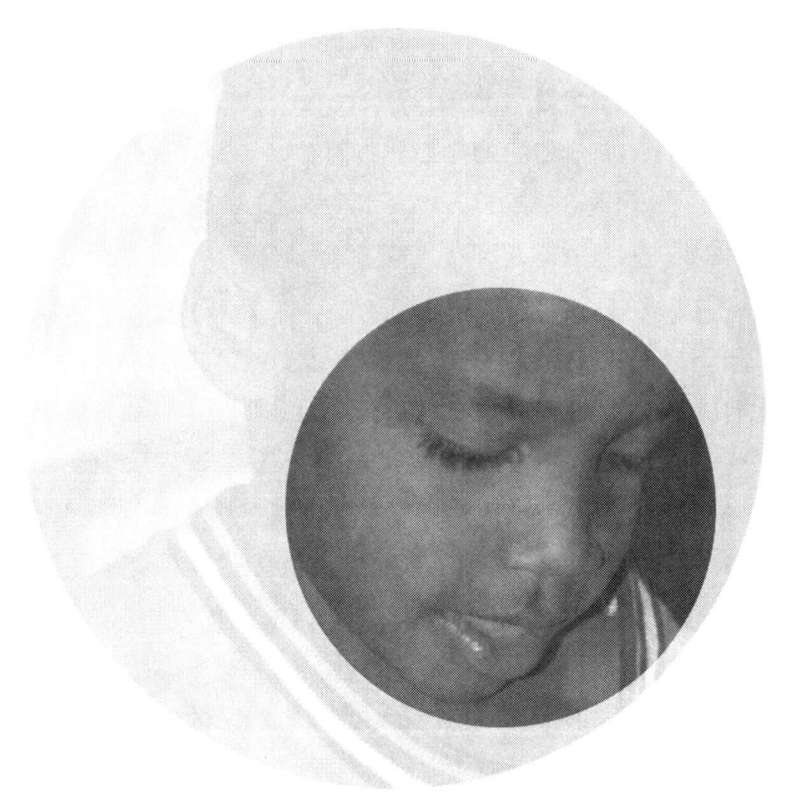

DECEMBER

Teaching Pre-K?

I remember the first time my Program Director, Mark Williams, from Teach For America approached me about teaching pre-Kindergarten. I was riding in a car with a fellow corps member and I thought the reception on my cell phone was failing me. It wasn't.

"I'm sorry, you're breaking up ... did you say pre-K? As in four-year-olds?" Needless to say, I had mixed feelings. I did not yet understand the importance of teaching students before kindergarten. My mind filled with visions of temper tantrums, bathroom accidents, and an endless stream of tears. I thought about my own pre-K experience and could remember only a difficult transition from home to school and the sheer disappointment of attending "Romper Room"—which, contrary to my initial assumption and hope, was not in fact the site of the joyful 1980s television show, but, rather a small, unpublicized nursery school on Long Island.

On top of this general reluctance, I felt a deep anxiety about stepping back into the classroom after my first experience as a corps member. I was initially placed in a fourth grade position at a K–8 school in Newark. My good intentions, Georgetown diploma, and overall relentlessness failed to translate into strong leadership for the students in my class. My principal ultimately decided to release me from my school and recommend that I be transferred to another school in the district after just three months in the classroom.

I did not feel ready for this second attempt at teaching, this second chance. From the moment I cracked open Teach For America's training materials during the spring semester of my senior year of college, it was clear that high expectations for my students were vital to facilitating their growth. I still believed wholeheartedly in their abilities, but could not say the same for my own potential as a teacher. Self-doubt threatened to paralyze my efforts to persevere as a teacher and leader, and I feared that this would prevent my students from mastering crucial foundational skills and realizing their own potential.

Luckily, perseverance won out. I would teach again, and this time I would find a way to succeed. I was determined to succeed.

The support of Teach For America's Newark regional staff was pivotal in mentally preparing me to reenter a Newark public school with the necessary confidence and vision. Regional Program Directors are a critical part of Teach For America's support structure for corps members during their two-year teaching commitment. Regional Program Directors are former teachers who, after being successful in their own classrooms and demonstrating skills needed to lead other teachers, support about 35 corps members through classroom observations, one-on-one conferences, and constant efforts to help their corps members identify and pursue additional professional development opportunities. This description may be helpful as a job posting, but it fails to describe the full scope of actions Mark, my regional Program Director, took to foster my growth as a teacher.

JUNE 28

Not a Coddling Mentor

I knew even before I met Mark in person that he was serious about his job. His attention to detail permeated everything from his communication about my teacher certification courses to the Newark regional guide he provided that described various neighborhoods in Northern New Jersey where I might live. He approached each of our interactions with a high degree of professionalism and expected nothing less of the corps members he supported. Most of us were recent college graduates who came directly from school to the Newark region for induction and would be living at Fordham University during our summer training institute. Mark was quick to make it clear that Teach For America would in no way be an extension of college. We were now professionals who would be held accountable for our work with children.

As a manager, Mark understood the power of knowing your audience and communicating accordingly. He knew that a corps member having a tough time might need a few minutes of lighthearted conversation before talking about classwork. He knew that sometimes it takes a half hour chatting with a district human resources bureaucrat to make sure a teacher's paperwork is processed in a timely fashion. In short, he was amiable, but professional, and always able to get the job done.

Mark's unrelenting commitment to his teachers and the Teach For America movement as a whole was evident from the start. I truly grasped what this meant during the last night of my summer training in the Bronx.

JULY

Reflections on Mark and Training at Teach For America's Summer Institute

I had a tough time at the summer training institute, both with my teaching of middle-school summer classes, as well as my ability to collaborate with the other three corps members with whom I was teaching on a rotating schedule. The diligent student in me that had wowed professors with well-crafted essays quickly mastered the art of designing a five-step lesson plan. My fledgling management skills, however, undermined any chance these plans had for successful implementation. Teach For America stressed the importance of strong classroom management and provided concrete strategies for developing routines and procedures that would make things run smoothly. Long before I even stepped foot in my summer school class, I had read about these strategies, observed them in action in several classes in Newark and New York, and written out the details of systems I would use. Yet when it came time to stand in front of the class and use these systems to teach, I grew tense and unsure of myself. When things did not go according to plan, I was not flexible or assertive enough to bring the class back to attention. All I saw was a failed plan, hours of preparation wasted. All I felt was exhaustion after staying up until three in the morning, finishing graphic organizers on chart paper. I went to bed without enough physical energy to wash the orange-marker stains off my fingers, though not too tired to feel a rush of anxiety about teaching in just a few hours.

In college, I could go home and sleep after pulling an all-nighter. Now I had to pull myself together, control my nerves for the 10 minutes I had to scarf down my breakfast, get on that bus, and teach.

Mark saw all of this when he came to visit my class. He maintained a stoic demeanor to avoid disrupting or upsetting me further. He sat for about 10 minutes and left a note on the back desk. As the class abruptly left the room for lunch while I scrambled to collect the Venn Diagram assignments a handful of the students had completed, I was both curious about the note and deathly afraid of reading it. The large block letters spelling out TEACH FOR AMERICA on the stationery reminded me of why I was there in the first place, and made me feel queasy considering just how disappointed I was in my teaching performance. Mark's words, however, offered both comfort and hope. "Ms. Pappas—Thanks for letting me stop by. Nice job on the agenda to keep them focused. Hang in there. We'll talk later—MW." "NICE JOB ... HANG IN THERE ... WE'LL TALK LATER." I went through the rest of the day's sessions eagerly anticipating some helpful advice that now outweighed any concern of a critique that might hurt my feelings.

JULY 26

Toward Understanding and Competence

Our appointment was at 7p.m. Mark was finishing up with another meeting, and the room was filled with other first-year Teach For America corps members from about five regions. These teachers were problem solving with their program directors, discussing everything from how to check for understanding in the middle of a lesson to revisiting classroom procedures to how to collect assignments in ways that will increase efficiency and reduce behavioral disruptions.

Mark finished up and could tell I was not up for sitting in a room buzzing with collegial exchanges. He suggested we talk outside. We sat on the steps and began talking about my experiences in the classroom, my time as an undergraduate, and my workaholic/perfectionist tendencies. I barely looked at my watch because we became so engaged in a discussion about time management, confidence, and what it means to be prepared each day to teach. Mark listened attentively and challenged me to redefine my approach to success. If I were going to stand in front of a group of children each day ready to implement plans and, at the same time, respond to unexpected occurrences, I needed to be more efficient with my planning time, assert myself as the leader in the classroom, and have the management systems and overall composure to maintain control of the class. He listened carefully and shared more about his own classroom experience, including modeling a few examples. He said that becoming a strong teacher is a process and that this would be the beginning of an ongoing dialogue. He didn't once look at his watch, but as I started to feel my eyes grow heavy I glanced down and noticed that three hours had passed. I felt tired and still not entirely confident in my abilities as a teacher, but much better, nonetheless. As Mark said, this would be the beginning of a process towards excellence.

As I returned home, I felt like I was transitioning from a place of confusion and helplessness towards one of understanding and competence.

NOVEMBER

Still Stumbling—The Process Continues

I came back from Thanksgiving break feeling defeated and exhausted and without a teaching position. Once again, Mark was there. He said that the Newark team should be able to find me a new job, so I should come by the regional office and be ready to move forward. Mark saw in me a commitment to professional improvement that he believed would translate into positive results for a group of children in Newark.

13

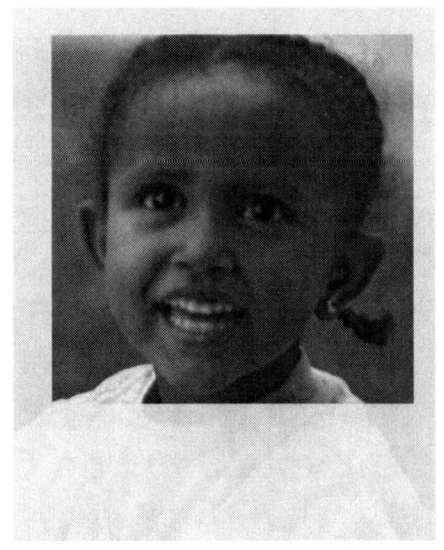

DECEMBER 3

Out of a Rut: Stepping Back to Reflect on Leadership

As Mark and I walked towards the Teach For America office, we started to talk about leadership; well, leadership and the caramel macchiato I was going to buy for Mark to thank him for coming to see me.

Once he got his caffeine fix, Mark and I got down to business: the business of my rebirth as a Teach For America corps member. Knowing my interest in politics, Mark said, "Think about the strong leaders you know on Capitol Hill and in history. What are they like, especially in difficult circumstances?"

I reflected on leaders past and present working to advance unpopular reforms that often conflicted with prevailing attitudes. They didn't allow obstacles or resistance to defeat them. In fact, those challenges further fueled their momentum. They maintained their composure, worked tirelessly to help others, and forged ahead to advance their cause. I needed to do the same.

FEBRUARY 27

One Step Closer to Pre-K

The process of finding and securing a new placement took several months, but eventually a pre-K opportunity came. I then had to apply my developing understanding of strong leadership to my preparation to meet the needs of young learners. I needed to move beyond my initial reservations about pre-K by understanding more fully the stakes, prospects, and challenges involved. I began to read more about early childhood education in low-income communities, particularly in New Jersey. I soon learned that if I embraced the idea of introducing my students to the importance and benefits of school, I could set the tone for how they thought about themselves, their peers, and the adults in their lives. The prospect of being the first person to greet students at a classroom door, ever, seemed both intimidating and empowering. Mark, with his own experience as an excellent kindergarten teacher, helped me see it as the latter. He noted that in his own classroom he could tell which students had gone to pre-K by their comparatively stronger listening and early literacy skills. And with the Abbott programs in our district making pre-K education available to all children in the district, either in school settings or Community Based Organizations (CBOs), these students were not just the ones with particularly involved families. Mark assured me that I would not just be "skimming the cream." Mark's insights, coupled with my own observations of pre-K and kindergarten classes in both my inner-city district and a nearby affluent suburb, highlighted the critical role I could play in closing the achievement gap as a pre-K teacher.

MARCH 2

Happy Birthday Dr. Seuss and Ms. Pappas: A Pre-K Placement at Last

I learned that it is one thing to want to teach pre-K in Newark, but it is another to secure a placement. And it is yet another thing to start teaching at that site. While reaching Community Based Organizations (CBOs) was difficult, partly because so many people seemed to be in charge, I ultimately connected with a CBO that had Abbott pre-K classrooms funded by the state. I went through a phone interview, an in-person interview, several weeks of emailing back and forth, as well as a handful of scheduling mishaps with a woman whose email address ironically started with the phrase "Make It Happen," before I secured a final interview.

Mark was glad to hear I was moving forward with the placement process. I still had mixed feelings about my abilities as a pre-K teacher as I got on the bus and rode up Clinton Avenue towards the center. My thoughts went back and forth between a positive image of myself working with young children as they actively explored materials, and the terrifying prospect of failing to create a highly functioning and productive classroom. The only distraction that calmed me down was to count the number of churches along the way. That worked, and by the time I arrived at my destination and rang the bell, my nerves were partially at ease.

The ninth church that I counted housed in its basement the pre-K program for which I was hoping to work. Because I was eager to keep the ball rolling, I arrived early, and had to wait about twenty minutes before the interview. In the meantime, I saw several families pick up their children. It was Dr. Seuss's birthday, so the children that passed by all had tall red and white striped-paper hats on their heads, not to mention large smiles on their faces, just the kind of looks that you would expect to see on a four-year-old coming from a special celebration. The joy was clear and, as anyone who spends any time with preschool-aged children knows, so pure and palpable, that it even made an anxious, self-defeated young teacher forget about her challenges. Well, at least until the Executive Director said, "Come on in, Ms. Pappas."

The Executive Director was at first a bit skeptical of my intentions. When I referred to my past experiences as a teenager working with young children in my own neighborhood, he asked, "Would you approach your work with our students with the same tenacity?" I remember being shocked because—for one thing—my time spent with young Greek-American children in an affluent suburb consisted of babysitting, informal story time, and the occasional art project. I explained to the director that it seemed obvious to me that students coming to pre-K already at a disadvantage would require committed teachers prepared to give them *more* attention and targeted instruction than students in higher income areas who typically come to school with a stronger foundation of cognitive and language/literacy skills. In short, children in low-income communities didn't need equal treatment, they needed something more, otherwise they would always be struggling to catch up. My strong opinions helped overcome some of my lingering anxieties. I demonstrated my commitment both by conveying these views and sharing the written plans I had prepared for the class. In the end, the director appreciated my enthusiasm and gave me the job. He even let me come by the center to observe a typical day before I actually started teaching.

MARCH 9

Ups and Downs: The Journey Continues

On my observation day, I was all set to stay the entire day and start setting up my room after the children left. That morning, I met some of the children and started to take notes about their skill levels, interests, and personalities. Soon after, the director abruptly came in and told me I had to leave because some officials from the state were coming in to inspect the center. He said they would call me and that I would most likely still be able to start on Monday. An hour later, I received a call from the center saying they were very sorry but because of financial circumstances, they would not be able to hire me at this time. Soon after, Teach For America-Newark's Executive Director came into the office to see if we had heard about the state discovering significant financial mismanagement at a number of centers in Newark. Apparently many centers, including the one where I was going to work, were using Abbott funds to support non-Abbott programs within their centers (for example, centers could offer daycare at their site in addition to state funded pre-K).

Luckily, I was able to find another job at a school for the fall a few months after the first job lost its funding. Nevertheless, the experience of seeing financial mismanagement take my job away and negatively affect the educational opportunities of so many children was an important lesson about one of the variety of ways in which children from low-income communities can be put at an educational disadvantage.

AUGUST 20

The Wheels on the Bus

I remember sitting on the New Jersey transit bus, anxious to see my school and start setting up my room. As the bus pulled out of Newark Penn Station, through the downtown area on Broad Street, towards the South Ward of Newark, I started to wonder what my future students were doing in their last few weeks before the start of pre-K. The appearance of my room and my approach to these children and their families would shape their first impression of school. What did they expect? What prior experiences with adults and other children would they bring to my class?

As I sat on the bus, contemplating the mindsets of the 15 four-year-olds who would be my students, a man next to me looked at my large crate filled with cleaning supplies, alphabet charts, and bulletin board decorations, and asked, "You a teacher?" I overcame my hesitation and responded, "Yes, well I will be soon." He then asked if I would be teaching in Livingston, a higher income suburb at the end of the bus line. Unlike his first question, I responded to this one quickly and without hesitation: "No, in Newark at Carter Elementary

School." His eyes widened as he leaned back in his seat and said, "Wow, really, are you serious?" I suspected some reference to my age or race would follow, but instead he exclaimed, "I went to Carter Elementary School years ago! Is Ms. Smith still there? She was mean." Just then a young woman chimed in, "You had Ms. Smith too? Yeah, she used to call me out, but Ms. Jackson was real nice." I told them this would be my first time at the school, but I would see if those teachers were still there. The man then peered out the window, noticing that the stop for Carter Elementary School was approaching and said, "Oh, here's the stop." We then left the bus together.

As the 70-bus to Livingston pulled away, I saw a small church on the corner, a corner store in the distance, and individual houses lining the street, one of which my bus partner entered after saying goodbye. I also noticed a man sweeping garbage off the street. He did not wear a uniform; he just seemed to be a resident intent on keeping the neighborhood clean. As I walked away from him and closer to my school, the litter seemed to get worse. I wondered how my kids would view school if garbage lined the entrance to the building.

AUGUST 20

A Classroom of My Own

I had planned to ask a series of questions about the school and discuss my "School Preparation Action Plan" (an extensive list of preparation steps I would take to ensure the classroom and I were ready for the first day of class) with the principal, but her hectic schedule of meetings in preparation for the first day of school prevented any kind of lengthy discussion. At one point, I happened to walk into her office as she was instructing the custodial staff to clear the garbage away from the area surrounding the school. I was relieved to hear that the garbage was going to be removed, but now I was too focused on what my room would look like to keep thinking about the exterior of the school. My principal then asked one of the vice principals to give me the keys to my room and told me the paper for my walls was all the way down the hall. Then the principal left for an appointment downtown. I didn't really know what all this meant, but I was determined to budget my time in the next few weeks to familiarize myself with the school policies and set up my room so I could feel sufficiently confident on the first day of school. And if I was not 100% ready, I needed to be okay with that; rather than panic and risk losing control of my room, I needed to focus on being present and proactive in the way I interacted with my students. My "School Preparation Action Plan" coupled with a focus on readiness was a big step away from my paralyzing lack of confidence.

The vice principal walked me to my room, gave me my keys, and said, "Well, this is it. I'll be leaving in a couple of hours, but don't hesitate to let me know if you need anything."

The sight of furniture and toys strewn haphazardly throughout the room coupled with the unfamiliar curriculum texts overwhelmed me. I soon found solace in my detailed "School Preparation Action Plan." The kids would arrive in less than three weeks, and I had to ensure they found a safe, clean, exciting, and print-rich classroom waiting for them.

> *A "print-rich" environment means that there are plenty of print materials in the class (such as books, magazines, newspapers, menus, recipe books, and so on), labels on various pieces of furniture, and signs or posters, many of which the children would ultimately help make.*

The walls were a drab purple hue with a chipped and coarse surface that showed its age. I looked down at my action plan and saw, "make walls bright and inviting" as one of my tasks to be completed. The thick, humid August heat that filled the air of my classroom must have blocked my memory, because I could not recall anything my principal said about what to do with the walls. I wandered through the building, looking for someone who could provide some direction. Luckily, a veteran kindergarten teacher was just around the corner, putting the final touches on her room with the help of her three daughters. Her walls were bright and cheery, but not from a fresh coat of paint. She used rolls and rolls of fadeless butcher paper and, from what she told me, I needed to do the same. I spent the next few days covering my room with bright yellow, green, blue, red, orange, and purple paper with the assistance of two new coworkers. One was another veteran teacher who was already finished with her room, the other was Ms. Franklin, a 70-year-old teacher's aide who thankfully was not shy about telling me when I did something wrong. In the end, I had a swollen hand from the constant banging of the staple gun, but my room looked more like a place where a four-year-old would want to play.

AUGUST 23

Beyond the Paper-Covered Walls: Making Room 111 a Conducive Learning Environment

Next on my list was to create a safe room arrangement, one conducive to an active and age-appropriate pre-K day. I enlisted the help of Mark, who not only brought with him years of experience in early childhood education, but also a better sense of spatial relationships than I could ever hope to acquire. We moved wooden furniture (tables, chairs, bookshelves, play ovens, blocks, and more) and a large alphabet carpet around the room. Despite the 95-degree heat, the extreme humidity, and the lack of air conditioning, we worked until the arrangement was just right. In a pre-K setting, this means:
- Separating the quiet areas such as the Library, Writing, and Science Centers from noisy areas such as Blocks and Dramatic Play Centers;

- Putting messy areas such as sand and water near a water source;
- Providing space so children and adults can walk freely in between and around furniture;
- Making materials accessible to children at eye level; and
- Ensuring that adults can see the children at all times.

AUGUST 24

Tables and Relationship-Building

The next day I learned that despite the effort Mark and I invested in the arrangement, I failed to consider another crucial element: the opinion of my teaching assistant, Ms. Morrison. Her friend and colleague, Ms. Souter, came in to relay a message: whatever I did with the room I had to make sure the large kidney bean-shaped table was in the front of the room by the door so that Ms. Morrison could serve the breakfast and help greet the families as the kids entered the room each morning. The news initially frustrated me, particularly when I considered the hours of work and sweat Mark and I had put in the day before, and the fact that Mark would not be able to come back to my school because he was helping other corps members. Yet when I thought more about the specific request, and considered how important it would be for me to develop a strong relationship with Ms. Morrison, I decided that changing the arrangement to suit Ms. Morrison's request, while requiring more time and energy, would be the best move for my students. In pre-K, being the lead teacher does not mean being the only decision-maker in the classroom. You certainly have to assert yourself with the students and sometimes make the ultimate decision if you and your assistant disagree. Nevertheless, I needed to develop an open and collaborative relationship with Ms. Morrison so my students and I would benefit from her years of experience.

Ms. Morrison's priorities prompted me to rethink the rationale behind other choices in my room and, more broadly, the meaning attached to the physical space teachers and students would enter in just a few weeks. The positioning of furniture serves practical functions, the safety and productivity of my students being central. I also needed to consider other messages sent to students and families as they first stepped into and then proceeded to work and play in the room. How would I convey to students and families that this was first and foremost a space for them? I was the leader of the classroom, but this was a place designed to serve my students' needs and maximize their time in school. I therefore included the following:

- Blank space for student artwork in the Art Area with the title, "Our Works of Art" and individual frames where I would later put the students' names.

- Additional space, at children's eye-level where possible, for student work throughout the room.
- A section of the classroom library for "Students' Favorites," which would include books the class ultimately decided were their favorites.

> This space was certainly important for the students and families, but, given that students' artwork often does not take the form of a two-dimensional drawing or painting of a certain limited size, we later made space for other kinds of art forms: during the fall we created a pumpkin museum with individual small pumpkins the students decorated with paint and other materials. We invited family members, administrators, and other teachers to view the exhibit.

- A bin in the library called, "Pre-K 111's Books" for books the class makes, an idea I learned from a Teach For America alumna teaching kindergarten who often made big books with pieces of construction paper or oaktag. She used shared, guided, interactive, and independent writing to make the books with the students and bound them together with metal book rings. The books covered a

wide range of learning objectives including basic concepts of print, letter and word awareness, and, if tied to a particular theme, science, math, or social studies objectives linked to that theme. The books also gave students a sense of pride and ownership of their work knowing that they were authors and, as authors, completed a piece of work that is just as worthy to be in the classroom library as a book by Donald Crews, Bill Martin Jr., or Denise Fleming.
- An inviting author's chair in which students would sit when presenting their writing (or drawing) to the class.
- A Family Board for information about the instructional focus of that week, invitations for special events in the classroom or school, photographs of family volunteers (for example, reading to the class) with the title, "What's the Buzz in Pre-K 111?" at the front of the room.
- An envelope at the entrance of the room with a pen and notepad paper for administrators or other teachers to leave notes or other paperwork in order to avoid distractions during the instructional day. At my old school and the schools of my colleagues, other teachers and administrators repeatedly interrupted lessons with non-urgent messages and paperwork. I wanted to send the

message that while I am a respectful professional who will address any concerns they have and comply with all administrative requests in a timely manner, my primary function is to serve my students.

My time spent before and after school in my classroom also helped me take advantage of opportunities for productive learning time. I was responsive and diligent when it came to working with other teachers and administrators and preparing my classroom materials during that time so that I could be fully present for my students between 8:25 and 2:55pm.

- Clearly identified space on my desk (a letter tray) for any paperwork I needed to complete or submit in order to stay on top of administrative requests and not waste instructional time
- A place on the carpet for each student, marked with masking tape
- Supply-kit cubbies—one for each student, filled with basic supplies (such as glue stick, thick pencil, chubby crayon, stickers, and so on), with their names on each supply, the supply kit, and the cubby itself

AUGUST 25

The Teacher's Desk and Leadership

I could not figure out where to put one piece of furniture—my desk. The teacher's desk—that wide clunky desk I recalled from my elementary school days as the place at which my teachers sat while we completed our work—was a symbol of the separation between teacher and student. I wanted to take a different approach: whether my students were reading independently on the rug, eating lunch, or at centers, I wanted to be present as an active participant in their learning process. I did not want to give my desk a position of prominence in the room. At the same time, I wanted family members to know that I was fully accessible to them. From talking to other teachers, it seemed as though family members typically associated the teacher's work with her desk, so a desk far away from the door may suggest that the teacher does not consider visitors a crucial part of her work. Given this perspective and my other efforts to maintain a student-centered room, I decided to situate my desk near the door. I still felt unsure about the implications of this move, but part of being a strong leader, as Mark taught me, is that not everything is going to be perfectly aligned with your broader vision all the time. Often, you have to make a decision and move on instead of belaboring a particular issue. Lingering on such a decision can potentially undermine the operation of the classroom as a whole. I decided that I needed to be decisive and open to the possibility of changing the arrangement at a later date. Although I still valued the process of intellectual deliberation, as the leader of my classroom, I needed to curb those inclinations and move on.

AUGUST 25

A First Encounter

One day, as I was preparing the room, one of my future students came in with his stepfather. Jakim seemed a bit hesitant, but he eventually came in—his hand tightly clasping that of his stepfather. His eyes widened as he surveyed the brightly colored room, with a wide range of exciting materials just waiting to be explored. Jakim gravitated towards the transportation toy bin in the Blocks Area, carefully selected a red sports car, and rolled it across the floor.

"He loves cars," his stepfather remarked. I began to ask Jakim about his interest in cars, but he was still a bit too reticent to respond. I remember thinking back to that day in late

August several months later when Jakim anxiously entered my room each morning with a wide smile on his face that seemed to proclaim, "I feel excited to be in school because you are here!" My first interactions with many of my students were similar, as were my subsequent reflections on their growth.

AUGUST 31

Preparing for the First Week of School

As I continued to prepare my room, a second grade teacher came by my room to welcome me. She warned me to get ready for the "Hurricane of Tears," a.k.a. the first week of teaching pre-K, with many students who have never been to school. Her "weather" advisory made me think about ways to make the transition to school as smooth as possible. I wanted the kids to know that school is fun and exciting, and that coming to school did not mean permanently removing themselves from their home environment. I decided to include opportunities for the students to talk about their families and make artwork for their loved ones. On the flip side, I also wanted to establish some continuity between their work at school and their experiences at home at night and on the weekends. I set up a "Family Lending Library," which included individual library cards (see sample on page 188), and put together homework project packets including a "Quiet Zone" sign to designate a place in their home for students to read and do projects with their families. As for the

tears and potential bathroom accidents, I discussed standard procedures with Ms. Morrison who, with years of valuable experience, was able to provide some helpful tips:
1. Nurture the children while helping them make the necessary adjustment to life away from home. A quick hug and redirection to the focus of the larger group can go a long way.
2. Set boundaries with families. While some children need more support during their transition to school, all students need to be able to redirect their focus to classroom activities.

This second point is especially tricky. Family members who linger make the transition more difficult, both for their own children, and the other children in the class, who see these family members but cannot be with their own. We needed to devise strategies for communicating this to family members sensitively, so that they know we want them to be actively involved in their child's education, but that in the first few weeks there can be a downside to their participation in the classroom. I responded by providing information about a host of ways they can be involved, both in person and in our "Welcome to School" packet, and by letting them know how they could say goodbye and encourage their children to move on with the day's activities.

SEPTEMBER 4

Planning for the Big Day

As I moved forward with planning before the start of school, I considered my vision for the class, including the messages I wanted to convey to students and their families through my classroom environment and interactions with them.

These key messages included:

- School is an exciting place where you can make friends, be successful, explore and learn new things, and have fun; and
- You are safe here to play, explore, express yourself, and take risks as learners.

I envisioned a class in which students:

- Followed daily routines and procedures with confidence and ease;
- Were genuinely engaged in lessons and daily explorations, confident in their abilities, curious about their surroundings, and excited to learn.
- Progressed significantly in all developmental domains (cognitive, social/emotional, lan-

guage, and physical) to the point that they were more than ready for kindergarten. This means that they would be able to:
- Resolve conflicts with their peers using their words,
- Listen attentively to their peers and adults,
- Express themselves verbally in full sentences and with an expanded vocabulary,
- Comprehend and ask questions about stories and compare/contrast the experiences of characters to their own, and
- Demonstrate foundational literacy and math skills.

Foundational literacy covers a wide range of skills including print awareness (for example: concepts of print such as print moving from left to right and that the print tells the story, letter and word identification, and different functions of print), listening skills, oral language development, phonological awareness (such as rhyming skills, identifying beginning sounds in words), and emergent writing skills (such as writing their names, basic high frequency words such as the, like, and is, writing for different purposed including during play, and starting to write sentences using

> *high frequency words, their names, and invented spelling). Foundational math skills cover a wide range of skills including one-to-one correspondence, rote counting, addition and subtraction with concrete objects, making patterns, seriating and sorting objects, using math comparative terms such as "more and less", and identifying numerals, shapes, and colors.*

I knew that if I wanted to achieve this vision for my classroom, I had to gear everything I did with and in preparation for my students—starting from day one—toward achieving these long-term goals. This was especially clear to me after all the talks I had with Mark and after my time in the Teach For America intensive summer training institutes, where I learned to view teaching as leadership, as well as the deepening sense of urgency I felt after observing the other pre-K classroom in Newark the previous spring. In response to all of this, I developed lesson plans for the first few weeks that would reflect this broader vision.

SEPTEMBER 4

Crafting an Early Childhood-Friendly Schedule and Approach to Families

Another thing Ms. Morrison and Mark stressed was the importance of factoring my students' short attention spans into how I approached teaching them. Mark suggested looking at the daily schedule like a series of mountains and valleys—the high points being times when I would require my students to give me more of their attention and the low ones being periods during which students had more freedom to explore and learn on their own. Those "down times" did not, however, mean that I would have minimal interactions with the students. While the students would be away from the circle in centers like Dramatic Play or Art, at meals conversing with their friends, or outside during gross motor time, my knowledge of their strengths, weaknesses, and interests would guide their independent exploration time in a way that fostered their growth. This was certainly not a college classroom. To be honest though, even a lecture on the rise and fall of Rome by my professor Amy Leonard would have been more engaging had we explored the topic with blocks, sand, or playdough.

After I took Mark's advice and began to break down the day in chunks of time and to define those periods in terms of how I would maximize learning time, the day as a whole seemed more manageable and productive.

For the morning, this meant that in whole group or circle time we would follow our morning routines of breakfast, student sign-in, and independent reading. After the students and I had morning meeting at the rug, they would go either outside or to the cafeteria for gross motor time, and occasionally they would participate in a special art or gym activity outside of the room, depending on the day. I would then lead the class as a whole on a brief tour of the centers, after which the students would be free to choose a center in which to play and explore. A small group of children would meet with me, and then go on to the centers while I moved through the room, recording anecdotal observations and interacting with children to promote their learning.

> *Gross motor time refers to the period of the day during which students engage in activities that strengthen their gross motor skills (a.k.a. large muscles—arms and legs). In some schools and community-based organizations, this time is spent on some kind of playground. Many public schools in Newark, however, don't have a playground, but just a cement yard fenced in for recess time. We therefore have to bring portable equipment such as tricycles, balls, and hula hoops outside or in a large open indoor area such as the cafeteria or the auditorium.*

In addition to all this time spent preparing for my students, I had to think proactively about how I would approach families. While most of my families already had other siblings in the school, the first day would introduce them to the world and culture of my classroom. I took seriously something Mark told me about working with families to get involved and invested in the early childhood educational setting: think about it—mothers, fathers, aunts, uncles, grandparents, whomever takes care of these young children are entrusting you with their children's lives. Up until this point, these individuals have been the children's primary caregivers—charged with the responsibility of ensuring that the child is fed, clothed, and provided with shelter. Now those guardians are allowing you to shape their children's first experiences with the outside world. I wanted to prove to the families that the time spent in my classroom would add tremendous value to their children's life trajectory—that not only would their children be safe, but that each moment spent in my classroom would help their children realize the potential their families saw in them.

SEPTEMBER 6

The First Day of Class (Classroom Setup Before the Students Arrive)

After several months of intense planning—time spent in my living room designing instructional and management plans, making posters, and sorting donated library books; time spent shopping in Staples, Duane Reade, and "99 Cent Dream" on Newark Avenue in Jersey City, checking off one item after another on my School Preparation Action Plan; and time spent in my school arranging furniture, establishing relationships with colleagues, and organizing materials—the time had come to introduce my students to school. But the morning I woke up to start teaching pre-K, I felt neither ready nor confident. Despite my intense preparation and conversations with Mark and other members of Teach For America Newark's staff, all of the fears and insecurities I felt in my prior teaching position reemerged. Contrary to the helplessness and hopelessness

I felt several months before when I left my prior teaching position, and then when I first heard about teaching pre-K, these negative thoughts did not prevent me from moving forward. I remember walking to the PATH station in Jersey City at 5:50a.m. with no one else around, thinking to myself, "I've got to do this."

That little pep talk I gave myself proved sufficient. I kept moving and did not stop until I reached my classroom for the first official school day. It was the first of 180 days of school and for each I would arrive at 7a.m., knowing that I had to be ready for anything. It wouldn't be enough to say, "I could have addressed that child's need, reached out to a student's family, or responded to my principal's request for some paperwork, if only I had more time" because extra time in my classroom was something I could control, period. At that point, I still had about 90 minutes before the students arrived. Luckily, I had Mark's voice in the back of my head to help me focus. He was saying, "You think you're nervous? What about the children who are leaving their moms, dads, aunts, grandmas, or older siblings for the first time? What about the families who have to trust a complete stranger with their babies? You're the leader, Sophia! Take charge and don't let it get to the point when you feel like coming back to my office crying. Your kids deserve more than that."

Okay, so I'm the leader, and a strong leader doesn't waste time. A strong leader doesn't have a panic attack. A strong classroom leader gets her act together before the students arrive because once the children arrive she must focus entirely on them and their needs, not on classroom set-up or preparation of materials. I was nervous on that muggy day in early September, but I had also thought about all of this before I walked into my school. My detailed daily action plan, with sections for each period of the day when the students were not present, reflected this mindset. In fact, I crafted the template as a whole with one simple rule for myself: If I worked on something while the students were present, something that could have been done before or after school or on the weekend, I was, in effect, doing the children a disservice. Similarly, if I felt overwhelmed by something such as setting up materials or completing paperwork, I needed to think critically about how better to manage my time and to work with my teaching assistant. Often, these changes entailed adding a section to my weekly or daily action plans, engaging Ms. Morrison in a discussion about our responsibilities at different points in the day, or ensuring that I had an educational song cued up on the CD player in case I needed to handle an emergency during circle time. Although I entered Teach For America with a strong sense of personal responsibility, Mark challenged me to handle the multifaceted pressures of being a teacher by developing stronger management skills instead of embracing a martyrdom complex. True, I needed to work constantly for the betterment of my students, but if I wanted to lead them successfully from September to June, and not end up feeling overwhelmed and defeated, I absolutely needed a clear plan and structured mode of execution. An eager but haphazard approach might earn me some compliments from my colleagues for working hard, but if it didn't translate into positive results for my students, it was useless. Since organization and management were not my strongest skills, cultivating them became a central part of my commitment to closing the achievement gap. Otherwise, I risked leaving the classroom a naïve idealist with good intentions but no real impact.

On the first day of school, this preparation involved making sure my students' nametags were ready—a rather simple procedure involving string tied by Ms. Morrison, laminated green construction paper frogs, and a black Sharpie marker ready to go in my fanny pack. The cubbies, similarly, had blank labels covered with clear plastic tape where I could write each child's name. These details are essential for four-year-olds who are just starting to make sense of their larger surroundings with unfamiliar pictures that they would soon learn are letters and words that carry meaning. As their first teacher, I was in the position to facilitate basic print connections or to squander the opportunity to empower my students with a foundational skill.

As I completed what I like to call "Operation Basic Literacy Connection," I glanced over at the clock and noticed it was now 7:45—leaving me a little under an hour to complete preparations. I also greeted Ms. Morrison who, unlike me, had years of first-day experiences to keep her perfectly at ease. This was, however, our first time introducing students together.

Teacher-Teacher Assistant Relationship-Building

Ms. Morrison and I had only known each other for two weeks, and while she seemed pleased that I put her table in the correct place, she managed to question every decision I made that differed from the decisions of previous teachers with whom she had worked.

With the benefit of hindsight, I can see that these conversations helped make me a better teacher by prompting me to reflect critically about my plans. Yet in those first couple of months, lingering doubts about my expertise in early childhood education, combined with my desire to develop a strong relationship with Ms. Morrison (and to leverage her years of experience), led me to adopt some instructional practices that were largely ineffective and inappropriate (such as having the entire class practice writing the same letter with pencil and paper the second week of school). The more time I spent in the classroom, the more time I spent discussing with Mark how best to meet the needs of the children, and the more time I spent outside of class reading about child development, the more comfortable I became with asserting my authority in the classroom. Similariy, I felt better equipped with a confident mindset grounded in firsthand insights and background knowledge. I developed a vision of excellence for my students, retained high expectations for my students, and used individualized instruction. Together, these factors would make the children more than ready for kindergarten in all developmental domains. If a past teacher's lesson plans and daily schedule inhibited the realization of that vision, I could not just go along with it to make my life easier. So, while we were almost all set for day one of school, Ms. Morrison and I still needed to work out the kinks of our relationship in order to maximize our time with the bright young scholars of Pre-K 111.

Although some pesky nerves continued to taunt my still-developing sense of confidence, I was able to stay focused largely because of the time and energy I had invested in the action-plan items I was now completing. I could efficiently forge ahead with the preparations for personalizing the children's supply kits, as well as arranging circle time materials at the children's eye level (our illustrated daily schedule and an alphabetized name chart with the first letter of each name written in red). I did not have to question the logic behind these setups because I had already spent a great deal of time crafting a vision and concrete plans that reflected the needs of my students and their families.

SEPTEMBER 6

The First Day of Class (Classroom Setup Before the Students Arrive—Breakfast)

Final item: breakfast set-up. At orientation, my vice principal assured me that some older students would deliver the breakfast to my room around 8:20a.m., shortly before my students arrived. When I heard this, I imagined the ensuing chaos and confusion as 15 four-year-olds entered my room for the first time while some fifth graders delivered the crate of food that Ms. Morrison would—after returning from her welcoming duties at one of the school's five entrances—lay out on her large table. I decided this was not the best way to start school each day, not for my students, their families, Ms. Morrison, or me. I responded to the vice principal's description of the standard breakfast protocol by asking him if I could pick up the breakfast. He said I would have to ask the cafeteria staff, so I took out my action plan for the following day and added

"Breakfast setup: investigate possibility of picking up food early." I discovered that the food is ready around 8:00a.m. each morning and that the cafeteria staff (led my Mr. Gregory, whose attentiveness to the needs of my class throughout my tenure I deeply appreciate) could consolidate my class's food, juice, and milk into one crate to make it easier for me to bring the breakfast to my room in one trip. That meant that by the time my students arrived, breakfast would be ready and Ms. Morrison and I could focus on welcoming children and families and attending to any unexpected occurrences (such as Jafis crying hysterically at the thought of separating from his mother). As I lugged the crate up from the cafeteria to my classroom for the first of nearly 540 times during my tenure at Carter, I was intent on the task at hand: delivering the food to Ms. Morrison as quickly as possible without dropping the cream cheese-stuffed bagel bites. The children were set to arrive in fewer than 20 minutes, and I wanted to be ready to greet them. In the end, it took no more than five minutes to get the food to my classroom. At that time, I could not have imagined the positive impact this one arrangement would ultimately have on my ability to increase my preparedness on a daily basis, as well as give me the time to establish a strong rapport with my students and their families.

In one fluid motion, I set the crate down and grabbed my clipboard. The clipboard held the daily action plan that I had followed since 7a.m., as well as the daily lesson plan detailing the objectives and activities for the entire day. I reviewed the entire plan, focusing primarily on the top section. It described essential messages I needed to convey and specific actions that needed to take place in order to facilitate a smooth home-to-school transition for the children and families. This was a crucial part of developing a structured and supportive classroom environment conducive to learning. For students who entered my room anxious about leaving their parents and the familiarity of home, I hoped that predictable routines, logical consequences, and varied opportunities for exploration, fun, and accomplishment would pave the way for them to be engaged members of our classroom community. There were details on my plan for everything, from showing family members and children where to put their naptime blankets to notes on how to teach my students the procedure for transitioning from the breakfast table to the rug for independent reading and morning circle time.

> *My experience with Jafis for the first few weeks demonstrated both the importance of striking a balance between transitioning students to the structure of school while also supporting them emotionally as they deal with separation anxiety and developing a strong support system with your teaching assistant. That balance eventually proved necessary, but could not on its own address the immediate difficulty of one screaming child running down the hall to be with his mother and a class full of other young children. Ms. Morrison helped calm down Jafis each day while I worked with the rest of the class. Jafis's mother also worked to ease the transition by having his sister drop him off each day.*

Having reviewed and highlighted key sections of my plan, I felt as ready as I'd ever be for the children to arrive. As the bell rang, I could feel my knees weaken, my heart race, and a small part of my brain flirt with the idea of running for the nearest exit. I took a deep breath, quickly reminded myself of the need to transcend my own fears, and smiled. This was it. This was my chance. I had missed my opportunity to have a real impact in the classroom on the front lines in our nation's fight against educational inequity once before. It wouldn't happen again. Period.

SEPTEMBER 6

Welcome to Pre-K 111

"Welcome to Pre-K 111! My name is Ms. Pappas, and I am so excited to meet you." The students and families seemed to come in a bit faster than I expected, so I could never calm down completely between arrivals, but I managed to buck up and greet each of them. I wanted my students to know that I was not there to speak *at* them or only to talk with their families, so I made sure to squat down to their eye-level to ask them their names. The details of that day are a bit fuzzy, but I do remember the wide range of emotions revealed through their eyes: from excited to frightened. This was my first glimpse into the children's uniqueness as individuals. They had been alive for only three or four years, but they each brought a host of experiences, perceptions, concerns, hopes, and interests to our class. Jocelyn stayed close to her father and barely looked at me. Her father had to tell me her name because she was too shy. Najiyah entered smiling, accompanied by three older siblings. She told me her name and its first letter as I wrote it on her cubby. Tears gushed out of Jafis's eyes and were soon smeared all over his face. He was not about to let me or anyone keep him away from his mother. He clung desperately to her as she motioned to walk out of the door. I allowed her to stay a few minutes while he got settled.

While Ms. Morrison and I maintained an aura of calmness and focused the rest of the class on how to open their breakfast packages independently and use their words to ask a friend for assistance if necessary, Jafis's mother helped acclimate her young son to school. He didn't demonstrate progress in preparing his breakfast independently or expressing himself verbally to receive assistance on that day. Yet with constant reinforcement of the routine in following days, encouragement from Ms. Morrison, me, and his mother, and because he saw how the rest of the class was able to follow the routine, Jafis eventually got there within a couple of weeks. Had I allowed Jafis's difficulties that first day to derail the focus of the rest of the class, or to cause me to lower expectations, we would not have been able to move forward with the important work of active exploration and learning. Ms. Morrison's guidance was critical in keeping both the class and me on track. To be frank, when I saw Jafis crying, and saw some of the other children struggling to adapt to pre-K, my first instinct was to rush to open their milk cartons for them to avoid an eruption of tears. Luckily for my students' developing self-help, social, and oral-language skills, I took Ms. Morrison's lead. She was nurturing and helpful to the students without coddling them. She taught them how to take responsibility and politely reach out to and respond to others with clear and modeled directions. In doing so, she helped me translate my vision of productive and well-adjusted students into a reality.

As for Jafis, his mother sneaked out toward the end of breakfast and said she would see him later. He cried soon after that, but with some soothing words from Ms. Morrison, Jafis soon calmed down. I saw him peering at the door a few times through the course of that first day, but by the time we gathered for morning group circle time he was fine, at least until the following morning, when we would continue the sometimes painful process of Jafis's initial transition to school.

As we proceeded to our first morning group circle time, I began to learn more about my students. As a whole, the group responded well to a rhyming song I learned from a former Teach For America teacher. In class, we used the song to teach everyone how to listen attentively on the rug.

The rhyme used straightforward, modeled directions that also reinforced the names of body parts and introduced rhyming words to my students. The students also responded to clear and genuine positive reinforcement that highlighted specific accomplishments. This generated a strong rapport between me and my students; they knew and could trust that I would acknowledge their successes with honest feedback.

A small group of children sat quietly as they adjusted to their new surroundings. Interestingly, most of the children lived in the same neighborhood but had never met each other before. While some had been in daycare with other young children, others were only used to being around their parents and older siblings. It was time for some official introductions.

In subsequent years, I would use another song that became a class favorite and perfect springboard for some solid early literacy lessons. On that first day of my first year in pre-K, however, we just went around the circle and said our names. Responses ranged from Isaiah, who stood up with his head held high and loudly proclaimed, "Hi, my name is Isaiah Wright," to Jocelyn whose murmur you could barely hear. I was certainly anxious to begin getting a sense of my students' levels of development so I could start meeting their individual needs with differentiated instruction. My experience in the following weeks and years, however, made it clear that the performance of four-year-olds on these first days of school does not always reflect their actual skill level in one or more developmental domains. A difficult transition from home to school can often cause children who have mastered certain skills to seem weaker in those areas. Jocelyn, for example, could identify more letters than anyone else in the class, but did not demonstrate her knowledge or interest in that area until the third week of school because she was incredibly shy and often cried for her daddy. Once she became more comfortable with her surroundings and with me, she jumped (literally) at the chance to explore letters. It was heartening to see her become so responsive to my efforts to build on that foundation of alphabet knowledge, and to begin learning about words and letter sounds. She showed the greatest level of excitement during center time, small group, and in one-on-one interactions with me. Her ability to engage in the whole group lesson on the rug, however, took longer. In contrast, many times children who had an easier time adjusting to school and who were quite vocal, such as Isaiah, ended up exhibiting weaknesses in other areas, such as print awareness (Isaiah could not hold a book properly), counting, and key social skills including sharing materials and listening attentively to peers and adults. Isaiah's excitement on the rug that first day introduced me to a young boy comfortable in new situations. But if I was going to do my job and adequately prepare him and all my students for kindergarten, I needed to watch and listen to each of them closely, throughout the day, everyday, to understand and to meet their needs in all areas.

SEPTEMBER 6

After the Meet and Greet: Adjusting to a Full Day of School

All things considered, the rest of the day went pretty smoothly. We had a few criers, as was expected. But with the combination of Ms. Morrison's years of first-day experience and the lessons I had planned to teach our procedures and to give my new students a chance to express themselves and explore our materials, we were on our way to building a strong classroom community. The classroom tour was a critical part of this journey. First things first: the students needed to practice how to use "walking feet," "listening ears," and "inside voices," especially when traveling as a group. I quickly learned the power of a healthy dose of silliness. I engaged many of my children by demonstrating quite dramatically what would happen if we did not follow those rules. Even the children who were about ready to tune out for a nap were amazed at the sight of an adult falling over herself and onto the floor—all in the name of structure. "Isn't that what walking feet look like? Can somebody show me? I see Mickey Mouse doing it on the sign, next to the words 'walking feet,' but I'm not sure." I then called on two students to step up and show us the way. "Oh, that is a lot safer! Now, let's all practice it as we walk around the room." The students then traveled from the entrance to the Dramatic Play Area where so many of them would, in the coming weeks and months, take on a wide range of roles, including doctors, grocers, waiters, mommies, and daddies. However, just showing the children the area was not enough. I wanted them to start thinking about how they might actively explore and use the materials. I used a prop to initiate the process.

"Ring, ring ... what is that noise? Where is it coming from? Is it the stove? Is it Jafis's shoe?"

"No, it's the phone!" the students responded, anxiously.

"Oh, let's see who it is. Hello, this is Ms. Pappas, how can I help you? Oh, Spongebob, we are busy right now, would you like to leave a message?" I turned to the class with a puzzled look on my face. "Mr. Squarepants wants to tell us something, but we have to move on to the blocks area. How can I let you know what he wants?" The children responded with an equally puzzled look. Isaiah raised his hand. "I see the hand of someone whose name starts with the letter I, yes, Isaiah."

"Just tell us teacher. I love Spongebob," said Isaiah.

"Well, I would tell you, but I may forget what he wants. I better write it down instead. What can I use to write it down?" Again, blank stares and, I'm pretty sure, a couple of unexpected tumble weeds making their way through my classroom. I then had a few options before I lost their attention:

1. Just pick up a note pad, solve the problem for them, and move on;
2. Tell them Spongebob will have to call back when they return to Dramatic Play on their own; or
3. Make one last effort to encourage the development of their critical-thinking skills: silliness.

I decided to go with option three.

"Hmm, how about using this apple to write on Sarah's head? Will this work?" As I picked up a plastic apple and tried to write a message on Sarah's head, I began to see my students, even the ones who had been spent a good portion of the morning in tears, perk up. I decided to continue trying to transcribe Mr. Squarepants' message until I had riled up an overwhelming majority of my class, even at the risk of sacrificing our "inside voices" rules, just for a few minutes. I wanted to generate curiosity and a sense of collective excitement while getting them to think on their own. Slowly but surely the class erupted in a chorus of "Nooooos" or "That's not right."

"Well then what should I use? I feel confused and sad. I want to write the message, but I don't know what to use." (A little modeling of I-statements with feelings words also helped. My class would soon learn that in Pre-K 111, it is okay to be sad, angry, confused, and frustrated, as long as you express those emotions with certain words, not fists, kicks, or tantrums.) At this point, the students all started pointing to a box of markers and crayons on the table.

"Oh, what are these? Let me see." As I picked up a crayon and started writing, they followed my every move and breathed a sigh of relief. Ms. Pappas had solved her problem, they had helped, and we could move on. But they weren't just going on to blocks, art, sand, and the rest of the areas as passive observers. They had started their journey as active explorers, thinkers, and learners.

SEPTEMBER 26

My First Observation—Anticipating Mark's Arrival

I remember feeling anxious when I signed up to have Mark do his first observation of my class. He had not seen me teach since my first unsuccessful attempt the year before. Over the past year, he invested countless hours supporting me with concrete strategies for my classroom, feedback on my vision and plans for becoming a better teacher, and with tough love intended to empower me with the confident and mission-driven mindset I would need to persevere. I knew he would still be there to help me grow as an educator and not to judge me, but I also did not want to disappoint him. I feared that anything less than excellence would make him feel that all those phone calls, emails, and in-person meetings were a waste of his time—or worse, a sign that I was squandering the unique second chance I was given to help improve the educational lives and futures of my students. I signed up for one of the earliest observation times, partly to circumvent an extended period of nervousness and partly to force myself to move beyond those insecurities as soon as possible so that I could more fully focus on my students' progress.

As always, I went over my plans for the day in the 90-minute period I reserved before students entered in the morning. This time, I needed additional time because my worries about Mark's visit inhibited my ability to concentrate. I must have read over the open-ended question I would use to start the day four or five times before feeling comfortable moving on to the next section of my plan. "How did you come to school today? How did you come to school today? How did you come to school today? How did you come to school today?" In college, I studied and understood complex political and historical phenomena, but because of my anxiety I was having trouble remembering this simple question. That experience further shaped my understanding of what it takes to lead. It wasn't enough and it will never be enough to design plans and know content. Leaders need the confidence and courage to execute those plans regardless of who is present.

Luckily, for my nerves and my students, the bell rang soon after. By this time in my first year, we had already settled into our morning routine. The structure and predictability helped not only my students, but also helped me get over the hump of morning jitters to ease into the school day. Jafis was also significantly calmer, particularly after we discovered the benefit of having his older sister, not his mother, drop him off in the morning.

The students came in, greeted me, and placed their belongings in their cubbies. "Sarah! I feel excited. How do you feel today?"

"Fine" said Sarah.

"Who feels fine? Does Dora feel fine? Do I feel fine? No, I feel excited, so who feels fine?"

"I do" said Sarah.

"Oh, then what would you say?"

"I feel fine" said Sarah.

"Oh, that makes sense. So what do we do next?" Sarah then found her cubby with her name on it, with the first letter in red and the rest in black. "How do you know that is your name, Sarah?" Sarah pointed to the S, made the/s/sound and moved her arm like a snake. "Oh, /s/, Sarah, like the/s/in "snake"! Give yourself a kiss on the brain."

I used these routines to teach and reinforce a number of key language and social skills. In this two-minute interaction alone, Sarah and I worked on listening, oral-language development, letter-sound connections, and print awareness, not to mention how this interaction helped develop her ability to adjust to the routines of the school day. I also made sure the expression on my face and the tone of my voice conveyed my genuine excitement to see each student every morning. I learned this from my mother, who consistently greets her loved ones each time they come to the door as if she hasn't seen them in years. I wanted my students to know how crucial they each were to the functioning of our classroom on a daily basis. It was not okay for them to miss out on the fun and learning, and their absence would make Ms. Morrison, their classmates, and me sad because their presence added so much to the room.

    I went on to converse with my students as they ate their breakfast and looked for letters in the newspaper. By this time, the students had learned that if they want to open their cereal or any other food container, they either do it individually or use their words to ask a friend. Some of the students, especially the shyer ones, still needed me to facilitate the process of reaching out to a peer. I saw Liana sitting at the end of our *Cat in the Hat* table, staring hopelessly at her unopened milk carton. She had three friends around her, but chose to peel off the "table" label and bite her lower lip in frustration instead of trying again or asking them for help.

"Liana, that milk looks delicious, and the calcium will make your bones strong. Do you need some help?" Liana remained quiet, but I could see her eyes begin to well up with tears. "Hmm, I wonder if there is anyone here who could help you. I had some trouble putting away all the cars in the Blocks Center yesterday and one of my friends helped me. Is there anyone here who could be a kind friend to Liana?" Jocelyn stepped up. She was still shy but demonstrated her willingness to assist by extending her hand towards the milk container.

"Wow, look at that! Jocelyn wants to help. Jocelyn, why don't you tell Liana that you want to help so she knows for sure."

"I'll help you with your milk" said Jocelyn. Liana slowly turned her milk over to Jocelyn without saying a word.

"Thank you, Liana, for letting Jocelyn help you. Now what could you say to Jocelyn to let her know you appreciate what she's doing, that you're glad she is helping you?"

Liana said "Thank you" to Jocelyn.

"Excellent work, girls! Thank you for being such good friends to each other!"

Milk opened ... mission accomplished.

SEPTEMBER 26

My First Observation—After Mark Arrived

As I directed my students to the daily sign-in book and then the rug for independent reading time, the loudspeaker buzzed and I felt as though the milk from my own cereal were curdling in the pit of my stomach.

"Ms. Pappas, Mr. Williams is here to see you."

"Okay, you can send him down, thank you," I replied, making a conscious effort to control the shakiness in my voice. By now, I had a strong professional relationship and friendship with Mark, but I still dreaded his arrival.

He came in, greeted Ms. Morrison and me, and then settled into a chair, ready to see how I was doing in my second shot at teaching. Soon after Mark arrived, I transitioned the class to morning meeting with the "Read, Read, Read, a Book" song Ms. Morrison had taught me. We went through the different parts of our morning meetings, some of which were prescribed by my scripted curriculum, and others that I had incorporated to maximize the learning time with my students. The greeting song went well, but as we moved on to a discussion about their responses to the sharing question, I could tell that not all the students were focused. Jafis started by extending his legs and then proceeded to roll around, tap his neighbor, and talk on his own. Abdul turned his body around and began reading a book, while Shakira played with her shoelaces.

I struggled to regain the children's attention, and felt discouraged by our inability to get to rhyme time after the morning message. I then glanced over at the clock and noticed it was time for gym. Mark said he would wait in the class for me to return. As we traveled through the halls and up the stairs, I wondered what he would say. The pessimistic perfectionist in me felt disappointed in myself and anxious to improve. I came back to Mark smiling and looking around the room.

"So, how do you think you did?"

"Okay, not as well as we have done on other days, the kids just weren't with me, and I had to spend too much time addressing individual behavior problems. I didn't even use our behavior chart because I was so disappointed...."

As I began to rattle off everything that went wrong, Mark listened patiently, but then responded with a comment I did not expect:

"Well, okay, but I saw something different. I want you to step back and think about the whole class, who was with you, when they were with you, and when you lost some students' attention. The truth is that you were engaged with all but a few students. How can you build on their enthusiasm to spark the interest of other students? In terms of losing students, break down each part of your circle time and figure out how you might be able to prevent the misbehavior. Remember, they are young kids who often need to release energy. How can you make sure the pacing, transitions, and mini-lessons in your morning meeting reflect this need? You are on the right track. You just need to think critically about what is working and use those strengths to address other weak points."

"Whew, yes, that sounds practical and manageable. I'm also really tired."

"Well, remember, this is a process. Do not stay up all night to try to make all these changes. Commit to the process of making improvements over time. Otherwise, you will get to the point where it all seems overwhelming and impossible. And that won't help anyone, not your students and not you."

Mark was right. This was not finals time in college. I was not pouring all of my ideas into a 20-page paper I would hand into a professor in a week. I needed to adjust my mindset and organizational habits to the task at hand. I would start with my positive approach to my students when I picked them up at gym, but lay out a plan for more substantive change that would span the weeks and months ahead that would include my students, their families, Ms. Morrison, and me.

Within a few weeks, my morning meeting reflected the changes Mark and I discussed. We were on the circle for about 20 minutes, but to the kids it was more like five mini-lessons with plenty of upbeat and engaging transitions that included everything from singing and movement to common phrases I would use to segue into the next activity. I continued to use the song "Read, Read, Read a Book," but added a countdown and whole-group ticket system that rewarded the class for being ready to go when I reached zero and finished saying the "hands and feet are folded" rhyme. I kept my students thinking at all times by using the first letter or sound in their names to call on them, rather than just their names. I anticipated misbehavior by engaging the class in movement activities that often reinforced emergent math or literacy skills or moved students around to different spots on the rug. Lastly, I balanced firmness with frequent injections of silliness. Luckily, the students were there to help me when I got confused and tried to write on their shoes and heads instead of the whiteboard. They were also quite fond of our classroom puppets. Susan the Squirrel and Lucy the Lion made frequent appearances and were great at teaching the students about conflict resolution. For some reason Susan and Lucy frequently had problems sharing and keeping their hands to themselves, but the pre-K 111 problem-solvers were happy to help.

If we did not have gym or another special activity planned for the day, we would move on to gross motor play after morning meeting. We typically started with a ten-minute whole-group lesson that incorporated movement and infused skills from other developmental domains (such as playing Simon Says with a designated number of movements, or playing "Goin' on a Bear Hunt" while using positional words such as "under," "over," and "around"). After that came 30 minutes of free-choice time in which the children had a wide range of options (such as throwing, catching, rolling, and bouncing balls, jumping rope or making shapes and letters with ropes, as well as playing games with alphabet or numeral mats). Afterwards, students would come back to class, I would give them a brief tour of the learning labs during which time they had to give me their full attention, refrain from touching the materials without my permission, and raise their hands if they had questions. They would soon have the chance to explore these areas on their own, but if I did not outline clear behavioral expectations during the tour and consistently enforce these rules, the students would not have an understanding of how they could use the materials in ways that were both safe and conducive to learning. Then we would gather back on the rug and the children would choose the labs they wanted to explore. Those students in small group with me would choose first and then come back to the rug. The rest of them would go to the labs of their choice.

We had come a long way, and it was still only the fall.

JUNE 15

No Longer a Novice

I learned a great deal about my students and myself as a classroom leader that first year of teaching. Although I started the year feeling insecure about my ability to facilitate the students' growth, my commitment to constant reflection and improvement ultimately enabled me to transcend those fears and serve the best interests of my kids. The following chapters, based on blog entries from my third year in the classroom, delve deeper into how I approached assessment, planning, and instruction. The entries in this section that outline my first year teaching, including the invaluable contributions of Mark and the other members of the Teach For America regional staff, laid the groundwork for developing these systems and methods of teaching, as well as the success I had implementing them.

Part Two

Growth and Goals: Insights from the Classroom and Beyond

Introduction

Debates on the appropriate focus of early childhood education, in my opinion, often suffer from a false choice between an emphasis on either social/emotional or language/literacy and cognitive skills. Advocates of pre-K programs that focus on social/emotional readiness often begin the conversation with reference to the whole child. Yet their argument frequently becomes an endorsement of programs that concentrate more heavily on social/emotional development than growth in the other three domains of child development, and then go on to condemn more "academic-based" programs, like "drill kill" approaches. Their complaint is that, while producing some short-term results, such programs can negatively impact children and leave them further behind in the long run. In the whole-child model, teachers respect the freedom of students to choose the play area, "center," or "learning lab" of their choice by guiding their learning without requiring them to produce specific outcomes at any given time. Advocates on the other side of the spectrum purport to offer cultivation of social *and* academic skills, but stress the need to lay a solid foundation of early literacy and math skills through more structured and objective-driven lessons. They criticize the more play-based, whole-child camp for relinquishing too much control over the direction and outcome of student learning, wasting a unique opportunity to level the playing field before students enter kindergarten.

As a pre-K teacher, student in a P–3 certification program, and workshop facilitator for other early childhood teachers, I have talked to individuals on both sides. We all seem to want what is best for kids, but in the midst of attacking one straw man after another, we end up committing a greater act of injustice against children: allowing inflexible, dogmatic views to prevent the students from a more practical approach that can prepare them for kindergarten in all areas of development.

Many first-year teachers with whom I have worked and talked describe struggling because they think they have to choose between preparing their students for kindergarten using a wide range of literacy and math skills or ensuring they are well adjusted to and excited about school. These teachers have had mentor teachers from their districts come into their rooms and rip down the alphabet, telling them it is inappropriate to expose students to all those letters, because the students are not ready to begin literacy learning. These mentors say that teachers should instead focus on helping the students learn how to get along with each other and develop and discover at their own paces. Others teachers who work to develop their children's emergent writing skills through a combination of student-directed fine motor activities (such as molding playdough to make sculptures or assembling puzzles) and authentic writing experiences (such as writing grocery lists using scribbles and conventional letters in the Dramatic Play Area, or practicing signing their names each morning) face administrators who demand that three-and four-year-olds sit in chairs and write their names neatly on lined paper.

I respond to these concerns by noting the critical role a print-rich environment and authentic, age-appropriate writing strategies played in my students' developing the abilities necessary to leave my classroom excited to learn, write, and explore. My students left with an understanding of why we write and read, and with the ability to write using conventional letters, invented spellings, and sight words.

The following entries, which developed from a blog I wrote for Pre-K Now, demonstrate how I advanced my students' growth in all areas by balancing structure with flexibility and teacher direction with student choice. These observations and reflections came after three months of working closely with my students and Ms.

Morrison. The dates start in December of my third year as a teacher because that is when I began writing the blog for Pre-K Now.

Becoming Friends and Active Learners: Social Growth in Pre-K

Introduction

Social growth is a critical part of pre-K. Many of my students had interacted mainly with family members prior to coming to our classroom. I had to think critically about how to facilitate their adjustment to school and constant interactions with their peers. As with other domains of development such as cognitive and language, students vary in the abilities they have when they come to school and their response to different teaching methods. Some students picked up on classroom structures, including our approach to problem solving, through whole group discussions and read alouds; others required more individualized attention. I needed to be prepared from day one with positive messages, behavior systems, and an understanding that the development of a highly productive classroom community is a process that takes time. The first few months are crucial for laying a foundation of rules, norms, and procedures for students. Not all of my students responded immediately, but nearly all of them demonstrated significant growth by December and January. Mark (my Teach For America program director) told me early on that I needed to have a clear sense of how children should act and react to various situations. The more in tune I was to each child's needs and my own expectations for student behavior, the more progress I saw.

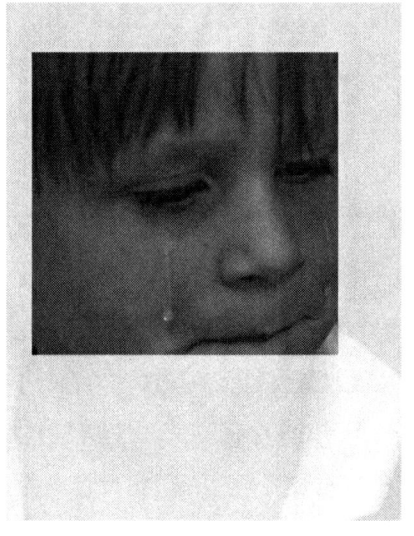

DECEMBER 6

Going Above and Beyond

    Yesterday, I saw David help another student for the first time. For the past three months, he consistently followed all the rules. He never disrupted the class or disrespected others. He listened attentively and cleaned up his mess. Yet, for the most part, up until now David has not gone above and beyond to help a friend.

    I aim to make my students not only "law-abiding" preschoolers but also individuals who respond proactively to someone in need. It is part of their developmental stage to focus primarily on themselves, but pre-K can also be a time when they become conscious of their larger surroundings and the importance of mutually supportive relationships.

    During circle time, we were all getting ready to crouch down like frogs and practice counting. David immediately squatted down but then noticed his neighbor, Tanasia, continued to sit with her legs crossed. He told her, "Come on Tanasia, you can do it. I know you can!" Without another word, she sprang up, ready to rib-it with the rest of us.

    We have spent months cheering on our friends when they come to the board to write or succeed in opening a milk carton after having difficulty. This was the first time David encouraged another student on his own. Way to go David!

DECEMBER 7

Making Peace

Karen and Tyrique had a breakthrough today. When I came to the rug after breakfast time, they and two other students were excited about the latest edition of a nature magazine. I responded by complimenting their enthusiasm and slipping in a little vocabulary expansion: "I feel so elated to see you getting excited about a magazine!"

The honeymoon did not last long. As I walked away to greet a latecomer, I noticed some of the excitement on the rug was turning into an aggressive and loud conflict over who would turn the pages. Camp David was not available at the moment, but we managed to devise a three-stage solution through informal talks on the rug:

- Two of the students would read the magazine for a few minutes while taking turns to turn each page;
- The first two readers would then peacefully hand the magazine off to the other two readers, with Ms. Pappas facilitating the transition; and,

- The second two readers would read the magazine on their own while taking turns to turn each page.

Through a fair "Eeeny-meeny" random selection process, Karen and Tyrique were chosen as the first two to read the highly coveted publication.

Well, mornings are a busy time, with math routines, morning announcements, newspaper letter hunts, and some anecdotal information collection before circle time. Sometimes I forget to go back to situations like the "Book Taking Turns Agreement." Today, however, my forgetfulness was not a problem. Out of the corner of my eye, I saw Karen and Tyrique walk over to the other two students, give them the book, and say, "Here you go. It's your turn now."

At that sight, I definitely felt elation. I quickly acknowledged their success by exclaiming, "Wow, I am so proud of Karen and Tyrique for being such great friends! I think today will be a purple day for you." Sure enough, they continued to cooperate for the rest of the day and were both put on purple, the highest honor on our behavior card system. If only international diplomacy were this simple.

This entry, first posted on the Pre-K Now website, attracted the attention of other educators with mixed feelings about my approach to and experience with behavior management.

One educator praised my efforts to engage the students in independent problem solving, but she criticized the use of a publicly visual color-card chart to track student behavior, calling it a system that would shame and discourage students. Another educator also expressed concern that such behavior systems are not developmentally appropriate for pre-K students.

My Responses

- Thanks for the note. I agree that students need all the encouragement we can provide. I also see how contagious it can be. Just today, my students were applauding each other without any prompting. I agree that behavior card systems can potentially have harmful effects, but I think my approach complements our emphasis on positive reinforcement and peaceful conflict resolution. As a class, we focus on the value of rising up and improving behavior, we encourage each other to make better choices, and we applaud students when they improve. We also admit that everyone makes mistakes and that we just have to pick ourselves up and keep trying to get to green or purple. Getting on yellow or blue does not become a permanent label because students are empowered with an understanding of how to get back to green or go above and beyond to reach purple. Plus, we all start off fresh on green each day. Lastly, I make a big deal out of students rising up but not on students going down to yellow or blue. I just flip the card without saying anything and move on. We thereby use our positive reinforcement as a class to encourage students while avoiding the labeling to which you refer. Thanks again for your interest in the blog.

- Thanks for your alternative point of view. I think behavior systems can be either appropriate or inappropriate depending on how one implements them. I think having a visual associated with behavior can help four-year-olds understand choices and consequences. Teachers may abuse this approach by using it as a way to judge or embarrass students in front of their peers. But I use it to emphasize student progress and, perhaps more importantly, the chance to improve behavior once you have dropped down on the color chart. Starting on green every day represents starting fresh. The message is "We all make mistakes. But we can think about our actions and do better next time." We also take time out to celebrate students who have improved, whereas when I am moving students down the chart I just move the card and move on. Moreover, the cards are not the only part of my behavior plan.

We take time to talk through our problems using I-statements and self-talk such as "I think I can," "Oh well, I'll get picked another time," and "We don't say, 'Oooooh.' We fix the problem." We use role-plays and stories to discuss social skills both proactively and as conflicts arise. The color card chart is, therefore, just one part of a larger management and culture system focused on positive reinforcement, consistency, mutual peer support, self-motivation, and developing an understanding of choices and consequences.

In my work with teachers since I wrote this entry, I have also stressed the importance of using color cards or any other visual representations as just that: a representation of meaningful positive and negative consequences that together help teach young students how to manage their impulses and become helpful and productive members of the classroom community. The concrete colors can help students as they navigate more abstract concepts like fairness and respect, but they should by no means replace the lessons about fairness and respect taught and reinforced throughout the school year.

This entry also prompted a new early childhood center director to ask some questions about assessments for behavior and academics in a pre-K setting:

One of the problems I'm having in developing a program to oversee, manage, and develop 25 new early childhood classrooms is the creation of a real assessment plan for behavioral and academic standards. It seems to be a practice from which new teachers in the pre-k setting would benefit immensely, but it also seems risky if not done properly. At some point, could you speak to the academic goals you strive to attain, as well as to how you measure for yourself the progress students make—and this speaks to your anecdote in this post—in behavior such as interacting and sharing?

My Response

Thanks for the note and questions. I use mostly performance-based assessments to measure progress and plan for meeting individual student needs. The goals are based on New Jersey's expectations for pre-K in literacy. I collect a variety of anecdotes and work samples each month that correspond to specific standards. I then use a detailed rubric for each skill to see where the students fall on a scale from 1 to 4. I also use checklists with specific skills for math and social skills. I take anecdotes throughout the month in order to make well-informed decisions for the checklist that reflect my observations over time. I hope this helps. Let me know if you want more details.

DECEMBER 16

The Horror of Sharing

Sharing space, sharing time, and sharing attention can be quite difficult for many adults—imagine teaching four-year-olds how to accept those realities in life! For my student Kevin, who exceeds most of the other students in academics, the idea of sharing is, simply put, horrifying. He breaks down in tears when he doesn't get picked for passing out the mats or if another child wants to play with the toy of his choice. As an only child being raised by his grandmother, he is not accustomed to sharing with other students. Yet now, as a member of our classroom community, he faces 13 peers, each with an equal right to the same toys and attention he seeks to hoard for himself.

Ms. Morrison and I consistently remind the class of the fairness and value of sharing. As the wise "philosopher" Dr. Pooh once said, "The more you share with others, the more they'll share with you." We do not give in when the anti-sharers cry. We provide plenty of opportunities for students to have special jobs and to explore our materials. We also facilitate discussions between classmates focused on how we feel when our friends don't share. And yet, Kevin's tears and wailing keep coming.

Last week we tried to invest the whole class in our sharing goal by introducing a message they could send to each other and themselves: "Oh, well, I feel sad, but I'll get picked another time." Results? Too soon to tell.

JANUARY 11

The Making of Problem Solvers

Ahh, the weekend. After exploring fantastical literary worlds for five days with old ladies swallowing flies, purple crayon-drawn hot-air balloons, and "wild things" at every corner, I get to delve into my weekly collection of non-fiction, "adult" content at a local café.

As I briefly step away from my pre-K teacher mentality to reflect on the latest news around the country and the world, I consider one unifying theme in each of the articles: problems. Regardless of your political affiliation, job sector, or daily blogger of choice, it is clear that current and future generations will face a wide range of political, economic, social, and technological problems. So what are we doing in Pre-K 114 to provide our society with proactive problem solvers?

One, we are creating a problem-solving culture in the classroom. Whether the problem is spilled milk, a friend crying, or someone saying they "can't" do something, we respond with efforts to fix the problem. Initially, the students said, "Oooh" and pointed instead. We then showed puppets in similar situations, brainstormed with the students about how to fix problems, and adopted the phrase, "We don't say, 'Ooooh,' we fix the problem."

We also do not give up. We learned from the Little Engine to keep chugging while saying, "I think I can," and asking for help from our peers. We receive positive recognition for going out of our way to help others fix problems. Students who got to purple last week included David and Tanasia for helping each other fold up their blankets after naptime, Awana for assisting Tyrone with his spilled juice, and Kevin for comforting Karen when she was upset.

A second step is to foster critical-thinking skills. Like my favorite adult publications, children's literature is filled with characters who have problems. We use these scenarios as a starting point for thinking about ways to solve problems. Here is an excerpt from a problem-solving discussion we had last Friday over breakfast, as we looked at a picture of Jack (of "Jack Be Nimble" fame) jumping over the candlestick.

> Ms. Pappas: What is Jack's problem?
> Sierra: His pants could catch on fire.
> Ms. Pappas: So what should he do?
> Sierra: Call 911 to put the fire out.
> Ms. Pappas: Great idea. What if he doesn't have a phone?

Tyrique: He could put his foot in the sink.

Ms. Pappas: Excellent idea. What if the sink in his house doesn't work?

Tyrone: I could take him to your house and put his foot in the toilet.

Ms. Pappas: How will you get to my house?

Tyrone: I will take a cab.

Ms. Pappas: What if I'm not home?

Ravon: He could take Jack to the supermarket for some water.

Awana: No, he not going to be on fire. He jumped over the candle. He was quick.

But it's not all storybooks and nursery rhymes when nurturing young problem solvers—we get them thinking about the world outside of Pre-K 114, too. I call their attention to potential problems such as running out of water or paper. We discuss why we need those things and ways to conserve them in our classroom. We are careful to keep the water on for five seconds while we wash our hands and to hit the paper towel dispenser only three times. The students then celebrate themselves for being "superheroes" and helping to save the world.

Now the only question is: which one of these great problem solvers in my class will join the presidential race next? Some potential frontrunners have frequently changed their mind on important issues (such as the *Green Eggs and Ham* vs. *Cat in the Hat* decision), while others have remained consistent, even when faced with opposition over how best to manage the number of people at the Computer Area at a time. Despite one candidate's initially strong position in the polls, her overly candid bashing of Mr. Squarepants, recently aired on YouTube could hurt her with the small, though well-organized "large pineapple under the sea" vote. Only time, debates, and exploratory committees will tell....

JANUARY 15

Reflections on Batman and Madam Speaker

"Girls can't be line managers, only boys."
"Ms. Pappas, he called me a girl!"
"Ms. Pappas, can my mommy be mayor too?"
"I don't watch Batman. That's for boys."

A few times per week, I hear my students make comments or ask questions related to gender. They are aware that some of us are girls, some of us are boys, and, depending on lessons taught at home and through the media, they bring certain preconceived notions about gender differences to the classroom.

While he could not clearly articulate the rationale behind his feelings, the boy who angrily approached me after someone called him a girl clearly felt insulted. And the boy who declared that girls could not be line managers used a matter-of-fact tone that alarmed me.

By coincidence, as I was reflecting on these beginning sessions of Gender 101, I happened to be watching the unprecedented introduction of President Bush to Madam Speaker Pelosi at his State of the Union address. I kept wondering, did a four-year-old Nancy ever have to struggle to gain a voice in heated debates over who would control the sandbox on the playground? What role, if any, did her teachers play in convincing her that she has just as much a right as little George, Dennis, or Harry to participate actively in decision-making processes?

I consider it my responsibility to treat every child with dignity and respect and to teach my students to treat each other the same way. That teaching requires engaging students in a dialogue that fosters a deep and rational understanding of why discrimination of any kind does not make sense and is harmful. I consequently seek to challenge my students with responses that make them think about their developing views on gender.

In the case of the "he called me a girl" comment, I used a neutral tone and said something like, "Okay, are you a girl? No? So just let him know that and move on." In terms of the Batman remark, I said, "Well, I'm a girl and I love Batman. I love how he uses a rope to jump off tall buildings and save people. Is that okay? What would you do if you were a superhero?" The mayor comment came up during last year's mayoral elections when the students were able to "write-in" someone they thought would do a great job leading the city.

None of the official candidates were women, and many of the students nominated their dads or uncles. We responded to the "mommy non-nomination" with a conversation about what it takes to be a good mayor and why mommies, daddies, uncles, aunts, grandmothers, or grandfathers could get the job done.

What happens when a teacher's views on gender clash with those of families? I have seen plenty of family members scold their children for choosing items from our "Treasure Chest" that they claim are not "suitable" for either boys or girls. I have not confronted the families about my own views nor have any family members asked that I limit the choices available to their children. I wonder if there should be explicit conversations with family members even if family members have not openly confronted you.

When this entry appeared on the Pre-K Now blog, educator Kathleen O' Pray responded with insights from her experiences with gender issues, both as a teacher and throughout her life.

> I grew up in the time period when women could choose motherhood or a job. Even the jobs were limited to teacher, nurse, secretary, or sales clerk. When I started teaching, Free to Be You and Me was all the rage. This made me very aware of the comments on gender. I think your

approach works well and I have done similar things with my students. Recently, I bought tea sets for my students. We have a set in class that they all love. It has improved their social skills, such as sharing. The language that the students use during these tea parties is rich and complex, and often extended. When I sent the first few tea sets home, I received a few negative comments from families of the boys. When I engaged the family members in discussion about the sets, the families became more positive. A number of them even went home and used the sets for a tea party. They were pleased how their sons and daughters behaved during these events.

JANUARY 20

The Rehabilitation of an Anti-Sharer

Ahh, the end of story time, right after lunch and before naptime. This is a time when most of the students are relaxing, flirting with the decision to crash prematurely on the rug before retiring to the comfort of their individual mats. Or the students are contemplating the complexities of the literary masterpiece just presented to them; in this case, they are pondering the enigmatic cyclical nature of Laura Numeroff's classic, *If You Give a Mouse a Cookie.*

For Kevin, this point in the day used to be filled will anxiety, frustration, and sometimes even pure anger if I did not choose him to help me pass out the mats. Not anymore.

Unlike the other students, our key phrase ("Oh well, I'll get picked next time") did not work for Kevin. Ms. Morrison and I decided to individualize our approach to Kevin's struggle with taking turns and building on his visual learning style and interest in taking on greater responsibility. Each day, after we complete our post-story discussion, Kevin walks over to Ms. Morrison's table and figures out who should have a turn to distribute the mats by reviewing a list of his classmates who have helped over the course of the past two weeks. He then announces the person picked for the day to the entire class. Since we have developed the system, Kevin has not cried or thrown a tantrum once during this transition time.

We still have some difficulties in other parts of the day: for instance, if he is not picked during a discussion or game on the rug. The intensity of his responses has subsided, and he is better able to manage his anger without much direct attention from me. He will sometimes turn his back to the group to weep silently or just breathe deeply. He either comes back to the group on his own in a few minutes or responds to me praising others or engaging him with an interesting activity. He even occasionally uses our "Oh well..." message.

We have certainly made progress in working with Kevin and helping him understand how to continue to improve his behavior in the future. His ability to stay focused and calm even when he is not chosen or he does not get what he wants will undoubtedly help him grow both academically as a learner and socially as a member of our classroom community.

FEBRUARY 1

Bringing It Off

Ali, Ali, Ali ... where do I begin? First, I feel frustrated with shortcomings in my own efforts to develop a strong relationship with her over the past four months. While we have some days and weeks during which she responds positively to my attempts to engage her in classroom activities, I see little constant progress in her behavioral skills.

Second, I cannot help but feel frustrated with her. Ali has done well academically, but persistent obstacles to her social development make me concerned for her overall progress in the future. She frequently likes to "do her own thing," as Ms. Morrison calls it. For Ali, her own thing is pretending to be a dancing cheerleader, regardless of what the other students and I are doing. We focus a great deal on respecting each other by listening to friends and the teacher during discussions. Ali, however, frequently does her cheers while the other students are responding to a question or trying to focus on my lesson at the whiteboard.

In addition to using positive reinforcement to focus her on our class rules, I give Ali many opportunities to express herself freely, both within the context of our large group activities and on her own before the activities begin. I integrated her interest in dancing into our morning meeting by allowing the students to dance during our greeting song. We also frequently cheer the names of our friends (to the tune of "B-I-N-G-O") and we use cheers to learn our high frequency words (such as "Give me a 'T.' Give me an 'O.' What does that spell?" "To!"). I have also built in free movement and singing time right after naptime and before gross motor time. I tell Ali she can cheer and dance all she wants for a few minutes on her own, but then she has to join the group for a quieter activity.

Still, Ali chooses to "bring it on" at inappropriate times, literally, performing the cheers from the movie of the same name.

For a little while, these compromises worked. Lately, however, her disruptive behavior has increased. When I try to talk to her about choices and different activities for different times, Ali rolls her eyes and says that all she wants to do is cheer. She has even said, "I want to cheer. I don't want to learn." Positive reinforcement to keep her focused on the rug now works only sporadically. She more often looks away or down at her shoes.

I understand that cheering is her interest, and I really want to give her many chances to express herself. Yet if I allow her to "do her own thing" all the time, she will not only miss out on our lessons, but she will have serious difficulty adjusting to kindergarten where the teachers will most likely give her little or no time to express herself on her own.

I decided that Ali and I would develop an individualized behavior contract (see sample on page 187). Together we would discuss and develop a written agreement that addresses:

1. How her behavior adversely affects her ability to learn and have fun with her friends,
2. What appropriate behavior would look and sound like,
3. How we can work together to reach that goal, and
4. How we can use her interests to design an individualized incentive system.

FEBRUARY 2

Forging an Agreement

I entered my class the next morning with a sense of hope in the potential for Ali and me to move forward with her behavior management. Armed with knowledge of her interests and of her strong oral-language skills, I was ready to discuss with her a highly individualized behavior plan that would invest her more fully in her own progress.

I approached Ali while she was eating breakfast to say that I really enjoyed her cheering and wanted to talk about ways she could teach the class her creative and fun cheers. Her eyes lit up and she began to do a cheer in her chair. Had it not been for the tasty cereal and juice, I am certain she would have jumped out of her chair.

I asked Ali, "If you are going to teach your friends how to do your cheers, what do they need to do?" The puzzled look on Ali's face told me I needed to be more concrete. "I know, your friends can talk and laugh while you are trying to show them what to do, like this...."

As I showed her what that would look like, Ali's confused look quickly turned to frustration.

She shook her head and proclaimed, "No, Ms. Pappas. They need to listen to me!"

"Oh, really? What does that look like? Let's practice. This time I will be the teacher and you can be the students." Ali responded by showing me how to listen quietly. "Oh, I see. That makes much more sense. And I can see that you can do a great job staying quiet and listening while I talk. Have you been doing that during circle time?"

Ali responded, "No, but that's because I want to cheer and dance!"

"You can. There is time for that, but sometimes you have to do different things, like listen to stories. If you can be a great listener, we can work together on using more cheers and dances on the rug and in other parts of the day. You will also have a chance to teach those cheers to your friends. Does that sound good?"

"Yes."

"Okay, we said a lot. I'm not sure if I remember it all. What can we do so we don't forget? Hmm, yesterday in Dramatic Play my friend David couldn't remember all the things he wanted to buy at the store, so what did he do?"

"Ooh, I know. David wrote it down!"

"What a great idea. But how will we write it. Can we use our fingers or feet?"

As I pretended to write with my feet, Ali giggled and quickly went to the Writing Center to get a piece of paper and a marker. We have writing materials in all the centers, but the Writing Center was closest to us at that time. We then wrote down our agreement using interactive writing.

The sentence read, "I will listen to Ms. Pappas and my friends. I will get to teach my friends how to cheer."

We then both signed our names on the bottom and Ali's mother signed it that night. I made copies of the agreement and talked to Ali about her progress at the end of each day.

FEBRUARY 6

R-E-S-P-O-N-S-I-B-I-L-I-T-Y

Certain birthdays represent meaningful thresholds in our society; times at which our culture determines that we are ready to take on new responsibilities. After seeing Ali today on her birthday, I am beginning to think we should add the big 0–5 to that list.

Ali often has difficulty concentrating on group work and respecting others when they are speaking, but today I saw improvement. During clean-up time, I noticed Ali reminding her friends to put their name cards back. We all know that if we forget, we will have to wait a couple of minutes before going to choice time the next day. As Ali told classmates to "put your cards back and be responsible" with a singsong tone, I walked over and thanked her for being such a great cheerleader.

We decided, spur of the moment, on a new title that connects her affinity for cheering to the classroom activities: Responsibility Cheerleader. Her face lit up, and she smiled as she repeated the cheer while heading into the bathroom to wash her hands before lunchtime. I plan to apply variations of this role to other parts of the day, and think that if she takes ownership of the cheer and receives encouragement and appreciation from me, the new role could make her more responsible and respectful of her friends.

Ali also did a great job focusing during whole-group time on the rug, usually a challenging activity for her. When she did call out disruptively, I did not call on her. She ended up crying, because she did not get a chance to convey her thoughts. I consider that a breakthrough as it indicates she cared more about participating in discussions than in doing her own thing.

Now, I am not sure if it was a heightened sense of maturity on her birthday that led to Ali's super day or her mother's promise of a Princess Barbie birthday party in return for better behavior. So, I covered my bases and spoke with her mother about an individualized behavior contract, which I plan on creating with Ali tomorrow morning. As I have learned from experience, if we can isolate those behaviors we want to change and design rewards around a child's interests, the child, the family, and I can more effectively focus on specific problems and lasting solutions.

We shall see....

FEBRUARY 28

Accidents Happen

"David, why'd you do that? You're not my friend. I hate you!" As I heard these words, I could almost feel the anger reverberating through Kevin's voice and hands, now trembling and clenched in two tight fists. I also saw confusion in Kevin's eyes as he heard the crash and Kevin's immediate reprisal while David clutched the yellow plastic hard hat he was trying to grab when he knocked over Kevin's construction.

Just a few minutes ago, Kevin had meticulously created the structure to represent tall trees capable of accommodating the elongated necks of his favorite jungle animal: the giraffe. In his mind, the accident threatened the well-being of animals for whom he cared deeply. He defended the rights of these animals with fervor, but expressed his anger in a way that hurt his friend's feelings and demonstrated an inability to distinguish between intentional and accidental harm.

A Note About Observation Notes: Putting the Accident Example in Context

I discovered the details about Kevin's thoughts by asking him to explain what happened, not by drawing conclusions based on my own inferences. It is important for teachers to take objective notes on student behaviors and interactions and not to impose their subjective opinion and analysis. Even if I had seen Kevin playing with giraffes before the incident, I still could not assume that he was confused by David's actions because of his attachment to giraffes. I wrote down exactly what I saw and heard during the incident, and when I asked them to recall what happened. I included the part about Kevin looking confused here for dramatic purposes and because of what Kevin told me after the incident.

This series of events was a perfect storm for several learning opportunities, which, taken together, could advance my students' ability to interact civilly with others while also standing up for what they believed in. I chose to focus on the accident factor.

Let's face it: Accidents happen. In my pre-K classroom, which is just a tad too small for 14 students, two adults, and 10 interest centers, accidental bumps and collisions are practically part of our daily routines. Most of the students have learned to cope. For a few students, however, these encounters can still distract and quickly escalate into an over-dramatized response. Aside from constantly reminding them "accidents happen," and facilitating problem-solving discussions and role-plays around the issue, I am not really sure what else to do.

When this entry appeared on the Pre-K Now blog, Kathleen O' Pray's response about conflict resolution in a pre-K class was:

> I think that helping students resolve these conflicts is one of the most important things teachers do. I so often see incidents among students in older grades escalate from an accidental bump to a fight because they expect the worst. I teach my students that accidents happen. That rather than get angry they can change the situation by using their own voices. A child can say, for instance, "Did you know you bumped me?" This resolves a situation in a minute rather then allowing it to escalate. An escalation we too often see. I am a strong believer that teachers need to teach socialization

skills every school year, throughout the school year.

MARCH 6

Honoring Our Contract

She did it! After three weeks on her individualized behavior contract (see sample on page 187), Ali finally earned enough points to present a special cheering show in front of the whole class.

As she stepped into the spotlight, Ali was surprisingly shy, unlike her attitude when giving frequent, disruptive cheers at inappropriate times. This "command performance" cheer was a bit more subdued. As her friends cheered her on, her face brightened, and I could hear a sense of pride reverberating through her voice. She cheered while clapping out each letter, "A-L-I, A-L-I, Ali, Ali, I am Ali! Ali, Ali, Ali!"

When I shared news of Ali's show with her brother and mother the following day, the pride became contagious. Her family members smiled widely and seemed relieved that Ali was showing progress.

Ali's road to victory was not quick and easy. She initially responded to the point system just as she had to our whole-class color-card behavior system, asking me angrily why I gave her a one or a two, or a yellow or blue card instead of connecting her behavior.

As we had one-on-one conversations each day that focused on her specific behaviors and the number of points that corresponded with them, she began to grasp the relationship between her choices and the consequences. Towards the second week, I would ask her how many points she thought she earned for the day, and she could usually guess correctly based on her own assessment of her behavior.

What does Ali's behavior look like on the rug now? She usually listens to her friends and me attentively and rarely creates a disturbance by calling out. We, of course, still have our cheering moments, but these have become exceptions.

Perhaps best of all, Ali's behavior improvements have facilitated intellectual growth. She engages more actively in discussions during storytime, making predictions and thinking critically about how to solve the characters' problems. Just last week, she posed a "water car" solution to the problem in Leo Lionni's classic, *Swimmy.* After losing his school of fish to one deep-sea predator, Swimmy found another school of small fish that were so petrified of big tuna fish that they would not swim around the ocean. Ali's solution required the small fish to drive a water car out of the ocean away from the big tuna fish. Ali was so focused that she not only suggested the idea but also wrote "wtr car" on our solutions list without guidance from me.

Her behavioral progress and academic progress have gone hand in hand, and I look forward to more improvements in the months ahead. This is one contract that makes both sides of the table happy.

APRIL 3

Bad Behavior Solved, Not Made, in High-Quality Pre-K

I was concerned last week when a recent report linking childcare to later behavioral problems in children grabbed the headlines. I can only imagine the guilt and frustration that families who have children in such programs felt when they heard this news. But the reality is far from the "damned if you do, damned if you don't" picture painted in the media.

High-quality pre-K offers the chance for young children to learn how to express themselves appropriately in a wide range of social interactions, how to solve conflicts with peers, and how to function productively in a structured school environment.

The first thing my students learn is how to follow set routines. Many children come into class without any previous childcare experience. Their first week behaviors have included children leaving the class to run down the hallway laughing and screaming and others simply wandering the classroom unresponsive to my efforts to give directions. I consistently implement classroom procedures and routines designed to make the students capable of working on their own and with others.

By the end of September, the students had mastered routines covering everything from sitting on the rug to clearing away their lunch trays. They also knew what would happen if they did or did not follow our classroom rules, why it was important to follow the rules, and how to "use their words" to solve conflicts. Their awareness of what to expect, their desire to receive positive praise, their investment in our "we are all friends" classroom culture curbed negative behavior. Moreover, our emphasis on the rationale behind wise choices such as peaceful conflict resolution made the teaching more lasting.

Although families can teach their children about solving problems and behaving appropriately, pre-K offers the opportunity for young children to practice these strategies with a large and diverse group of their peers on a daily basis. Kevin, a.k.a. "the anti-sharer," who frequently threw temper tantrums when he did not get a turn at something, exhibited similar behavior at home. Pre-K gave Kevin the chance to practice working out problems with other children, a skill that will help him in school and at home. Moreover, we used our knowledge of his learning style (based on extensive anecdotes from his family) to develop an outlet for his negative energy and provide an opportunity for him to take ownership of the solution within the context of our daily routines.

High-quality pre-K offers motivated, capable teachers who can analyze student's behavioral problems and implement enduring solutions. Without such attention, behavioral and educational problems could become endemic. I believe that my experiences in the classroom, both my struggles and successes, illustrate the need for educators, families, and policymakers to support efforts to provide high-quality early care and education programs for all children.

APRIL 24

Peace in Pre-K and Beyond

The other day I was reminded of the importance of solidifying positive and peaceful attitudes early on in pre-K. I overheard a teacher reprimanding a first-grade student in the hallway for hitting another child. The teacher simply said, "You cannot hit her, it's not nice. Do you understand?" When the child did not respond, the teacher said, in a more abrasive tone, "Say 'yes'!" The child then said "yes," as commanded, and the teacher moved on.

I had to wonder how effective that child would be at solving problems on his own in the future. Perhaps the teachers the child had up to that point had not taught social skills effectively. Possibly he had experienced things that have undermined his ability to behave properly. The incident caused me to reflect on my efforts this year.

I start teaching our peaceful and empowering approach in the beginning of the school year. The process entails direct whole-group instruction through puppet role-plays, books about friends and feelings such as *Words Are Not for Hurting* by Elizabeth Verdick, and songs like "The More We Get Together." In these activities, we use consistent language such as, "I feel sad when you _____," asking the students to fill in the blank. Add to this many one-on-one, informal, teachable moments, and gradually the students gain an understanding of why they should use their words instead of their hands.

By December, my students were able to follow through with a "peace agreement." However, rather than having the students initiate these agreements, I played a major role in the initial stages of the process. Since then, the students have made even more progress, and now take ownership of the peace process from the beginning. For instance, David used to suggest that characters in our stories use violence to solve problems. "If the Cat in the Hat won't leave," David would suggest, "we should hit him on the head." After spending time modeling a peaceful and empowering approach to problem solving, David is more likely to recommend talking through problems. When we discussed recently how the farmer in Martin Waddel's *Farmer Duck* exploits the duck and refuses to do any work, David chose peaceful means over violent ones, advising the duck to say to the farmer, "Please, can you help me?"

Other students still require occasional reminders and encouragement, but their skills are clearly developing. Tyrone's first inclination during a recent read-aloud was to hit the animals that had stolen a character's fruit. After I asked him, "Do we hit animals or people?" he offered an alternative measure: "I would tell the animals that I won't ride them anymore." Similarly, Jeffrey came to inform me today that another student would not let him play with a certain toy. All I had to say was "Work it out on your own," and Jeffrey returned to the student to say, "I feel sad when you won't let me play with it."

Pre-K teachers—indeed, all teachers—have an obligation to teach conflict resolution in a way that empowers students to solve problems peacefully. I want my students to leave pre-K with the rationale and language needed to facilitate peaceful conflict resolution so that, throughout their lives, they will be able to avoid having communication devolve into the scolding that I saw that first-grader receive in the hall. By teaching such empowering communication skills in the pre-K classroom, it is possible to lay the foundation for a society that more closely embodies Immanuel Kant's vision of enduring peace that I studied in college.

MAY 16

A Listening Ear

All I have to do is turn on a cable news show with talking heads barking at each other to know how important it is for the young generation to learn listening skills. I work intensely with my students on developing their ability to listen to teachers and each other.

Like any other skill, I start my plan for listening skills by familiarizing myself with the state's idea of mastery. The NJ Preschool Expectation for listening is very comprehensive. In addition to following directions with several steps, students must be able to engage in a dialogue with others and express ideas from previous discussions and songs into play.

With these guidelines in mind, I try to design lessons that cover each component. These can be games explicitly dealing with following directions (Simon Says has always been my favorite) or with increasingly complex directions. When we do the latter, I walk students through directions during small group and one-on-one interactions before asking them to perform the activity or play the game on their own.

Story-time discussions are obviously valuable opportunities for students to strengthen their listening skills as they listen to the teacher read to them. Students can also work on listening to their peers as the class engages in a dialogue about the story. I make a point of teaching my students how to build on the comments of another student and respectfully offer alternative ideas by using phrases such as "I agree" or "I disagree." During a recent read-aloud of Giles Andreae's book *Giraffes Can't Dance,* Jeffrey noted, "I think the giraffe is gonna leave the jungle 'cause the lion's mean to him." Samar then responded, "No, he's not gonna leave. The other animals will be nice to him."

Students also show progress by incorporating ideas from discussions and stories in their play. After building a house in the Blocks Area, Fuquan told everyone to step back and then cried, "I'll huff and I'll puff and I'll blow your house down!" In doing this, Fuquan applied his knowledge of the *Three Little Pigs* to his independent work. Similarly, Ravon showed me a turtle moving slowly in the Discovery Area after we acted out *The Tortoise and the Hare* during Outdoor Play time.

As you can imagine, with 14 four-year-olds still coping with the transition to school, concentration on one's own family as opposed to new classroom friends and activities can sometimes dominate the conversation. For instance, one student, Tanasia, often had her family on her mind at the beginning of the year. She would make comments about her brothers and sisters, regardless of the topic of our class discussions. After months of working on listening skills and helping Tansaia become more comfortable in the classroom, she now makes comments and asks questions that are pertinent to the stories and conversations at hand. During a story for Mother's Day just last week, in which the mother is in a wheelchair, Tanasia asked, "Ms. Pappas, why she in the wheelchair?" Derrell demonstrated his own growth in listening by answering her: "I think she fell in the street and was hit by a car."

These skills build a strong foundation for my students as they head off to kindergarten, having gained an understanding of how to follow directions and recognize the perspectives of others in pre-K. Now if you'll excuse me, I have some "Hardball" and "O'Reilly Factor" to catch up on.

MAY 24

Coping with the Bad Days

Like adults, pre-K students have good days and bad days. How we as teachers deal with the latter can significantly affect our relationships with individual students, their academic and social growth, and our overall classroom culture. Just as we differentiate instruction to meet the needs of all students, we must also individualize our approach to motivating them. Karen, though upbeat and highly participatory throughout the day, periodically comes to school in tears, clinging to her grandmother. She is quite comfortable using writing and drawing as a creative outlet, so when I see Karen so upset, I suggest that she write a note or paint a picture for her grandmother during choice time. This helps Karen remain connected with her family even when she cannot be with them.

Her grandmother and I have also worked on stressing responsibility with Karen. I thank all of my students for being responsible when they correctly follow our morning routine as they enter the classroom. Karen's grandmother and I use the word *responsible* when we are trying to stop her from crying. This process usually takes a few minutes. She then calmly puts away her belongings, washes her hands, and is eating breakfast with her friends in no time.

Awana occasionally comes to school sobbing and feeling lethargic, particularly if she has been absent on the prior day, or if school is starting again after the weekend. If she says anything, it is usually only "I want to go home." Awana's mother is not as actively involved in helping me handle these emotional situations as Karen's grandmother is, and Awana does not use writing and art in the same way as Karen, so there is not an external activity that I can suggest Awana use to work through her feelings. Awana does, however, respond well to good old-fashioned hugs. I usually ask her how she feels, let her know how I would feel if I were in her position, remind her of our classroom routines, give her a hug, and send her on her way to "have fun and learn with her friends." Kevin or David sometimes will notice the situation and thoughtfully give Awana hugs as well, or say "We missed you when you were out, Awana."

Ali often arrives late and upset about something that happened with her brother on her way to school. Despite our daily "fresh start," she sometimes resumes certain behavioral problems she exhibited on the previous day. I am quite familiar with her love of cheerleading and use this knowledge to motivate her and encourage positive active behavior. I often greet her by cheering her name or asking her to help me out with a cheer for one of her friends.

Understanding and effectively addressing mood fluctuations is an important part of my job, and through this process my students gain self-confidence and the trust in me they need to be engaged members of the classroom community. When we as teachers succeed in this role, it helps to significantly diminish the number and intensity of disruptions and students are less likely to use negative behavior to get attention.

MAY 26

Recognizing the Power of Pre-K

I started teaching pre-K with some understanding of the value of early childhood education. Yet certain incidents that first year solidified my belief in the need for all children to have an enriching and supportive first year in school.

I experienced difficulty connecting with Abdul throughout the year. He demonstrated strength in basic literacy skills from the beginning, but was hesitant to take on new academic challenges and frequently conflicted with both his peers and adults, particularly when he did not get what he wanted. His negative responses ranged from hysterical temper tantrums to silent refusal to follow directions. One day in December, he expressed anger over the book we chose through a class vote by turning his body away from the group. I vacillated between engaging him directly and delivering a consequence or ignoring his behavior to let him know that his response would not divert our attention from the story. I began to read in an engaging tone and noticed Abdul slowly turn around. The characters, setting, and plot ultimately piqued Abdul's interests to the point where he re-entered our community. His transformation was a testament to the positive influence teachers can have on young children by introducing the captivating world of literature and the dynamic interplay between social and academic growth. The inviting nature of the book helped Abdul begin to tackle his difficulties adjusting to school by demonstrating the joy he could experience if he focused and listened attentively with the rest of the class. He also learned that even seemingly undesirable outcomes can have positive outcomes if you give them a chance.

Another student, Alan, started school ahead of the rest of the students in both academic and social skills. He listened attentively, participated regularly in class discussions, and used his basic understanding of letters and books learned from his older siblings to grow further in reading and writing. Nevertheless, by early December, Alan started to argue more with his peers, disrupt whole group discussions, and throw temper tantrums during small group reading and writing sessions. He also drew pictures of himself trapped in a building in his journal. I learned from talking to his mother that they recently had a terrible fire in his house, leaving the family members homeless and living with his aunt who had three children of her own. I responded by encouraging Alan to draw more about the incident and reached out to our school social worker to learn more about how I could help him. The social worker suggested I continue to draw with Alan, but take it a step further by engaging Alan in a discussion about how he might get out of the house. One day, after one of Alan's tantrums, we sat down to draw. He added details including other family members in the house. I asked Alan how he could help his family. He then started talking about and drawing himself with a hose and a cape. The art therapy transformed Alan from a scared and helpless victim to a brave and empowered superhero who saved his family from the burning house. Alan's behavior started to change after that and he finished the school year nearly on a first-grade level in key foundational skills. The strategies I used to help him cope with the fire are not entirely responsible for his progress, but they did increase his resilience to instability outside the classroom. Such tragedies can significantly affect impressionable learners who often do not yet have the words or reasoning skills to express their feelings in a clear and calm manner. Teachers and social workers can work with students and families to ensure these experiences do not put children at a further disadvantage.

MAY 30

Saying Goodbye

This time of year, the class begins the process of transitioning from pre-K to kindergarten. Ms. Morrison and I prepare our students for the move out of pre-K 114, including the reality that many of the adults and peers the class has come to know may not be moving on with them.

My class started this process earlier than usual, because Ms. Mills, the woman who comes each week to work with the students on social skills, had her last day today. Saying goodbye is not easy for many people, both young and old. How we handle goodbyes for young children can be particularly delicate depending on their emotional development and past experiences.

Here are some ways we facilitate the process in pre-K 114:

1. START EARLY

We leave enough time to prepare students, mentally, for change. We engage students in a dialogue, plan special events like the pizza party we had for Ms. Mills, and give students other outlets to express themselves. Our conversation with the students about Ms. Mills' departure began a week before she left, and we have already started our conversations about the larger transition to kindergarten.

2. Invite Expression of Feelings in Many Forms

Children, like adults, express feelings in different ways. For Ms. Mills' departure, we not only discussed our feelings but also wrote, sang, and danced about them, too. We focused the conversation on how we felt about Ms. Mills throughout the year, not just about our feelings about her leaving.

3. Integrate the Transition Processes into Other Aspects of the Curriculum

Thinking strategically, we incorporate "saying goodbye" activities into other lessons. For instance, we created a whole-class letter to Ms. Mills using interactive writing, we used watercolor paints to make a piece of art for Ms. Mills, and we read a book with similar "goodbye" themes to help the students practice relating the characters' experiences to their own lives.

4. Consider Individual Children and Their Experiences

Some children have a particularly difficult time with goodbyes because of their own experiences. Think proactively about how to help these children deal with their feelings. For example, recognize that some may not like to talk about their experiences in a large group.

As educators, we must ask ourselves what messages we are sending to students during transitions like these, and ask what the students are taking away from the process. My students have a sense that sometimes people we care about cannot stay and that it is okay to feel angry or sad. They also have ways of constructively dealing with those feelings, whether it is writing a letter to the person who is departing or talking about the fun and memorable interactions with that person. As they move forward to kindergarten and beyond, students will need these tools to remain calm and focused, even in times of change.

After this entry appeared on the Pre-K Now blog, Kathleen O' Pray shared her own ideas for facilitating these types of transitions:

> Each year we have a few students leave during the year. This gives us a jumping-off point to get ready for the end

of the year. I often talk about when they (the students) will leave me and how I might handle it. Because our students often change schools many times during their formative years it is important to start early and ease them into such changes.

Leadership in a Pre-K Classroom: Setting Goals, Building Relationships, and Managing Effectively

Introduction

Teach For America identifies strong leadership as central to effective teaching. While I understood this relationship conceptually from the moment I started reading the curriculum texts during the spring semester of my senior year of college, my experience with three pre-K classes revealed the truth and power of this approach. My growth as a teacher and the progress of my students because I:
- Crafted a vision for our success that included my students' growth in all learning domains;
- Developed long- and short-term plans to realize that vision;
- Invested families and others in our class and school community;

- Proactively incorporated feedback and best practices from others in my plans on an on-going basis; and
- Worked tirelessly throughout the year to reach our goals.

The transition from academic to classroom leader was a difficult and painful process. I had to transcend the realm of good intentions and "tried my best, but couldn't cut it" to reach the intersection of a clear vision of excellence and "work until the job is done." As Mark would say, feeling sorry for myself meant giving up on my kids. In the end, this transformation enabled me to promote my students to kindergarten knowing that they had a highly engaging and purposeful first year in school.

DECEMBER 8

Classroom Site Visits

Providing high-quality pre-K in low-income districts has a great deal of potential to "nip the achievement gap in the bud"; and the efforts of New Jersey (by way of a mandate from the State Supreme Court) to make pre-K available to all four-year-olds in low-income districts is certainly promising. Yet when I observed pre-K in Newark, at the suggestion of my program director, I did not always see teachers making the most of that critical year before kindergarten.

The Teach For America-Newark office often arranges for corps members to visit other teachers' classrooms during professional development days or days when Newark Public Schools are closed for vacation and surrounding districts or local charter schools are open. I was the only pre-K teacher so Mark (my Teach For America program director) helped me identify individual centers to contact and visit, but the regional program staff typically forms relationships with schools and teachers so that they can send groups of corps mem-

> *bers at a time. The district Office of Early Childhood also offers teachers the chance to visit other classrooms.*

At a center-based classroom I observed, students had a chance to explore their interests in centers (for instance, washing baby dolls in the Water Area while others built a house in the Blocks Area); and the teacher incorporated high-quality children's literature (such as *The Very Hungry Caterpillar*) into morning circle time. On the other hand, it was already late spring in a classroom full of four-year-olds, and the teacher's daily routines and technique for asking her students questions failed to engage the students in higher-order thinking skills capable of laying a strong foundation for future success.

More specifically, I noticed the following things:
- The teacher engaged the students in a discussion about *The Very Hungry Caterpillar,* but only about the foods the caterpillar ate, not about how the caterpillar's journey may relate to the students' experiences (such as eating various new or exotic foods), nor did the discussion touch on problem solving, such as how the caterpillar might get rid of his stomachache.

- A few students came up to the board to identify a letter in the morning message, but the teacher did not use that time as an opportunity to advance the child's knowledge of letters, letter sounds, and words. For example, she might have said, "Hmm, the letter S ... which friend in our class has a name that starts with that letter?"
- The other students seemed disengaged while one of their peers was at the board. The teacher did not make an effort to include all of the children by, for instance, encouraging them to cheer on their friend at the board, or coming up with other words that start with the letter S.
- Before heading to free-choice time, students found the individual "center sticks" they would use to identify the centers of their choice. These sticks had unique symbols at the top of them (a butterfly, house, ball, and so on) that the children used to identify themselves, but they did not also have the students' names printed on them.

> *Free-choice time, sometimes referred to as center time in pre-K, refers to a time in the day when children may choose to play in a wide range of interest or play areas, each with its own set of materials. While the*

> *specifics of these centers vary somewhat depending on the curricula, most curricula include the following centers or interest areas: Blocks, Dramatic Play, Sand, Water, Discovery or Science, Art, Toys & Games/Manipulatives, Library, Computers, Writing, and Cooking.*

- Students planned for centers by taking their sticks up to a work-choice board that had pockets for each center, putting their sticks in the center pocket of their choice, and then telling the teacher where they wanted to go. The teacher did not engage the children in conversation about which centers they wanted to visit and why, nor did she encourage them to use complete sentences when telling her where they wanted to go.
- The teacher interacted with students while they were in centers, but with simple questions such as, "Is that fun?" or "Is your baby going to sleep or stay up?" The questions did not invite the children to reply with answers that developed their critical thinking and language skills.
- The teacher also did not provide authentic writing and reading materials in the centers that she could have used to facilitate mini-lessons on how to use writing to make grocery lists, compose letters to friends, write

about a piece of artwork, label a block structure, or compose a song. In fact, in the two hours I spent there, I did not see any of the children doing any writing and reading on their own.

I approached these observations with a critical eye, not to judge the teacher I observed, but because as I planned to improve my own classroom, I wanted to ensure that I maximized each moment with my students.

DECEMBER 9

Site Visits—Observing Model Early Childhood Classroom Programs

Mark encouraged me to visit other early childhood classrooms, and he put me in touch with a woman teaching kindergarten in Newark, who had a model classroom for the Children's Literacy Initiative and a private school in an affluent suburb in New Jersey. These observations offered a striking contrast between the early experiences of low-income and privileged children in high-quality classrooms.

By observing the teacher who had a model classroom for the Children's Literacy Initiative I learned a number of effective ways to lead four-and five-year-olds toward academic excellence and independence within a highly supportive classroom environment. I saw kindergartners engaging in conflict resolution with their peers without teacher guidance. For instance, while children were working on their own and the teacher was circulating to work with students individually, two of the students began to argue over a card game in the Math Center.

Rather than running to their teacher for help or becoming aggressive, the students tried to work the problem out on their own, consulted the classroom "Conflict Manager" for guidance. This third-party arbiter, who was just five years old, mediated the dispute by listening to his friends, encouraging them to tell each other how they felt using I-statements, and then facilitated formal apologies. All three students then resumed their work. No other students were involved, and the incident did not take the teacher away from her time with other students. I imagined what these students would look like in three or four years after they had learned how to use their words instead of their hands to express themselves, and how to remain focused on their work. That "work" might look different in fourth grade (they might be writing four-paragraph essays instead of playing a card game to learn how to identify numbers and count objects). Still, it seemed clear that if students were to get to the point at which they could write those essays, they needed to develop a focused mindset and an ability to manage their feelings early on.

I also learned about performance-based assessment. In addition to engaging students in meaningful open-ended questions while the teacher circulated in the centers, she carried around a clipboard with an index card for each student. The information on the card was divided into four areas: social/emotional, math, language/literacy, and physical development. As she observed and interacted with the students, she took notes on the cards. She later used those notes to inform her planning. I would learn about and use more elaborate systems as a pre-K teacher, but this approach highlighted the value of tracking student growth in early childhood largely by watching the students throughout the day. Students at that young age, particularly in the beginning of the year when they are unfamiliar with their new surroundings, will often not demonstrate their full capabilities using more standardized assessments.

The private, affluent school I was visiting had a wide range of materials and teachers engaging students in meaningful conversations. I also picked up some great pointers for how to integrate foundational counting skills in everyday math routines and to reach out to the tactile needs of my students by creating "feely numbers" with a wide array of textured materials. That said, one thing surprised me—neither class had a guided reading program that started at the beginning of the year. I later learned that such programs were rare in the more affluent communities, but not in lower-income classrooms. The kindergarten teacher remarked that they slowly introduce guided reading in the wintertime for those students who are ready, but that reading was not a high priority. In contrast, my program director started guided reading with all of his kindergartners in Newark in September. Mark and I discussed the possible reasons behind the less rigorous approach to kindergarten in the affluent suburb. Given the knowledge of basic literacy skills that students who come into those classrooms and, possibly, the caliber of education across grade levels, perhaps this school did not feel obligated to provide a more structured reading program. The privileges afforded to these students from K–12 and at home may enable greater flexibility in the first years of schooling. I certainly did not have to visit the privileged private school to gain insight into the school readiness gap between the children from high-and low-income neighborhoods. A trip to the children's section of Barnes & Noble on a Saturday revealed children as young as two-and-a-half actively engaged in reading while their family members asked them questions and shared their insights.

I knew from conversations with other Teach For America corps members who were teaching middle school and high school that I needed to raise the bar for my students at the outset of their education. The weaknesses that my corps members noticed in their students in sixth, eighth, and tenth grades mirrored the deficiencies I witnessed in the Newark pre-K classrooms: students struggling to think and read critically and express themselves thoroughly.

I was determined to lead my students on a different trajectory. My students would leave my room each June knowing how to think through problems, listen attentively to teachers and peers, express themselves verbally and in writing, and with the foundational literacy skills necessary to begin reading. They would do all of this with excitement and a deepened curiosity to learn.

DECEMBER 15

Curriculum Connections

Noticeable growth in pre-K is all about making meaningful connections. The connections happen when a child links decisions about sharing to consequences, a letter she sees on a label to a friend's name, or a discussion about hibernation to the cave she built with blocks. The ability of children to link pieces of information together reveals their progress in a wide range of social and academic skills.

The approach and underlying principles of a pre-K curriculum can significantly influence a child's ability to form such connections and, in turn, the quality of pre-K programs. While many pre-K curricula seem similar because of a common emphasis on "learning through play," the structure and focus of those activities can differ dramatically.

The scripted program I used my first year teaching had weekly themes and daily activities laid out in extensive detail. On day one, I was handed everything I was expected to use in the classroom, from theme-related art activities to the specific questions to ask children during story time.

How closely was I supposed to follow the script? I distinctly remember an instance when my resource teacher from the Office of Early Childhood first applauded my open-ended and higher-level thinking questions used in a whole-group discussion and then instructed me to keep the manual in front of me to make sure I was following along. Well, I wasn't following along, but that's because the direction of my students' comments diverged from the script, which, though thoughtful, could not possibly contain a true understanding of my individual students' interests and backgrounds.

It turns out my resource teacher was often just as torn as I was between "following the script" and meeting the needs of actual children. She would say, "When that door closes, it's your classroom," but at the same time she would ensure that I fulfilled all of the curriculum's criteria.

The school now uses an unscripted program that focuses on building meaningful relationships between students, teachers, teaching assistants, and family members. We focus on developing activities driven by the students' interests, and on creating a structured but flexible classroom environment responsive to the children's diverse needs. I, of course, have to plan more, but my ideas come from observations and reflections of my students' skill deficits, strengths, learning styles, and interests. Their connections to the material and my teaching strategies produce noticeable growth.

For example, this week Kevin and I were in the Dramatic Play Area when I showed him an airplane ticket he could use during our topic study on transportation. Kevin said, "Wait a second, Ms. Pappas ... the airplane cannot go straight up. It first needs to roll on the ground fast and then fly up, like the goose in the book. He had to run very fast and then fly up too!"

"Kevin, that is a great connection to the book about birds! We read that book a long time ago. Give yourself a connection kiss."

The movements we first used to complement our initial discussions about geese and airplanes were evident in the hand gestures Kevin used as he made his point. In addition, his interest in both areas helped him to invest in the thought process necessary to build on prior knowledge to generate new ideas.

When this entry first appeared on the Pre-K Now blog, it did not receive comments, but informal discussions with other early childhood educators revealed mixed feelings about scripted curricula. My colleague from across the hall fully embraced the flexibility and student-centered approach of open curricula as opposed to more stringent guidelines, which, she argued, fail to meet the unique needs of specific groups of children. Farther down the hall, however, a former pre-K teacher now leading a kindergarten class said he found the more scripted approach to teaching curricula quite helpful, as he determined which lessons would be appropriate for his students. First-year Teach For America teachers whom I supported in professional-development workshops and one-on-one conversations frequently sought a balance between the two: the freedom to craft differentiated long-term and daily lesson plans that facilitated their students' growth in all developmental domains and some guidance on creative ways to introduce concepts and skills.

DECEMBER 18

Taking Charge

Teachers work hard to keep students focused and engaged during circle time. Given students' short attention spans, teachers incorporate plenty of songs, movements, and upbeat transitions to make sure those 20 minutes are productive. Today I decided to see how well the students knew our routines by stopping before each transition and asking them what happens next. I shrugged my shoulders exclaiming, "Oh no! I don't know what we are doing today. What should we do? Should we just sit here and look at each other until your families come to pick you up?" Despite the obvious attraction of a marathon staring contest, the students opted to take charge and suggest we look at the schedule. We then decided it would be a good idea to have a daily Schedule Manager to remind the class what part of the day comes next. What would I do without them?

When this brief entry first appeared on the Pre-K Now blog, it generated a number of responses focused on best-practice sharing. Various pre-K teachers from across the country shared their use of illustrated schedules, some of which were interactive, to maximize the learning opportunity for students.

DECEMBER 20

Creative Thinking, Simple Resources

Whoever thought one big brown box could prove so exciting for four-year-olds, let alone become a valuable teaching tool! Unlike other pre-K teachers in inner-city areas, I am fortunate to have plenty of funds for classroom resources allocated by the great state of New Jersey. Yet I have also learned that simple and inexpensive resources can offer learning experiences that are equally if not more rewarding than commercially bought toys.

This past week we explored boxes, and the students' creativity took off. They transformed plain cardboard from the school cafeteria, my apartment, and the apartments of several friends into everything from a house where they could live with their families and friends to an enormous hat for *The Cat in the Hat.* Their great ideas generated discussions about which parts of the house to add, common behaviors of famous literary characters (including those from *The Cat in the Hat* and *Caps for Sale*), and even what I can only define as a precursor to some intense union negotiations. When an imaginary hurricane destroyed my roof, the students' team of engineers said they could no longer work to repair it because the time was eight o'clock.

I can't wait to see what they do with old newspapers and bottle caps! Oh, the possibilities....

DECEMBER 21

Not Your Grandmother's Scantron: Assessments in a Pre-K Classroom

The first years of school are far too critical to waste time on ineffective strategies. Accountability in pre-K programs is therefore vital to the academic and social growth of our youngest learners.

The word "accountability" may conjure images of standardized exams and hours of tedious test prep—not exactly what we would deem appropriate for a four-year-old. So what do assessments and accountability look like in a pre-K classroom? Well, despite the obvious attraction of handing a four-year-old a multiple-choice test with 50 rows of neatly curved oval bubbles marked A to E, the reality is that assessment in pre-K is not that easy. Yet that does not mean accountability in pre-K is or has to be non-existent.

Four-year-olds do not always show you what they know. Their moods, interests, and developmental stages can affect their performances on a day-to-day basis. If they do demonstrate growth in a particular skill area, such as drawing a picture or responding to questions orally, the students certainly do not all do it in the same way. That said, if you watch and interact with the children every day, all day, while taking anecdotal notes and collecting work samples, you can have the data you need to chart growth, design properly differentiated lessons that meet the needs of all learners, and hold programs accountable. My students' words, actions, drawings, and singing are my multiple-choice answers.

Take Tanasia, for example. For the first weeks of school, Tanasia spent the majority of her day in one of three ways: silent, bawling, or asking repeatedly, "When is my mommy coming?" Our one-on-one interactions often incited desperate pleas for her mother. Then, in early October, I began to observe her making connections between the print around her and her friends' names during choice time. That is when I knew not only that she was starting to adjust and build relationships, but also that she was picking up basic literacy skills. She would point to letters on labels in the Dramatic Play Area and say to her friend Karen, "Look, it's the

'K,' like in your name." If I confronted her with a barrage of letter-identification questions, she would clam up and start to cry. I began to address more and more of those skills during choice time when she felt increasingly comfortable.

Last year, one of my students struggled with letter identification but masterfully used movement to act out stories or create his own. My extensive anecdotal notes reflected these weaknesses and strengths. I consequently decided to address his weaknesses with his strengths by working with the child one-on-one to create movements for each letter. We waddled like penguins for the letter "P," made elephant noises with a long trunk for the letter "E," and so on. I recently met up with him down the hall in his kindergarten class, at which point he pointed out a letter and made the movement we had devised.

When my analysis of the anecdotal notes revealed that Kevin, who had difficulty sharing with other students, was a visual learner, Ms. Morrison and I taught him the fairness of sharing using a visual approach that puts Kevin in charge. Ms. Morrison calls Kevin over to her table right before naptime. Kevin then goes through two sets of name cards: one of students who have handed out the mats in the past week and one with students who have not.

He then advises her on which student should have the job for today using the second set of cards and moves that person's card to the first pile.

JANUARY 16

Out of Her Shell

"Hello, my name is Tanasia from Pre-K 114. We will now sing Dr. King," Tanasia exclaimed, loud and clear, so everyone from grades pre-K through two could hear her.

She did it! After a tough transition in the beginning of the year, Tanasia slowly began to participate in classroom activities without much encouragement from her peers or me. Rather than repeatedly crying and inquiring about the time of her mother's return, she now focuses on a wide range of subjects including bears and cars. The more she shares with us in terms of her thoughts and interests, the better able I am to chart her academic growth. Her gradual progress culminated in her widely acclaimed introduction of our class performance during the school assembly commemorating the life of Dr. Martin Luther King, Jr.

Her other accomplishments during the past two weeks include:
1. Counting each of her friends for snack time in a clear and loud voice without skipping anyone;

2. Identifying and chanting out the letters in the word "like" in our modeled morning message for the first time; and
3. Choosing to read books to and with her friends rather than reading alone. Tanasia even encouraged a friend to read with her when she saw her friend crying.

As I reflect on her growth, I consider two major reasons for our success with Tanasia:

1. *Student-Driven Instruction:* We took the time to understand Tanasia's interests and provided opportunities for her to talk about and make things for her family. Our discussions at the rug, during lunch, and at choice time included plenty of open-ended questions that allowed Tanasia to speak openly about what was on her mind: her sisters, mother, father, and auntie. For instance, if the mouse ate cookies and asked for some milk, we learned about how happy Tanasia feels when she eats cookies and drinks milk with her sister at home. In addition, while Tanasia first hesitated to join her friends during choice time, she began to gravitate towards the Art and Writing Centers once

she learned that she could take home her finished products. Tanasia may have been physically separated from her family, but since she had the chance to talk about and make things for her siblings and parents, she still felt connected to them while in school; and

2. *Classroom Culture of High Expectations:* We consistently responded to Tanasia's crying with the expectation that she would eventually become more of an active and enthusiastic member of our classroom community. Rather than excuse her from class activities or call her family to pick her up, we taught her all of the routines and rules like the rest of the children. If she needed to cry when she first came in, she could, but she still needed to unpack, put

her Math Homelink journal (a notebook with a summary of math-related activities children do with their families at home) in the bin, wash her hands, and get her own breakfast.

When this entry first appeared on the Pre-K Now blog, it generated an interesting debate among a former teacher and social worker who is now a mother, a half-day kindergarten teacher in Los Angeles, and myself. The mother and former teacher/social worker expressed concern regarding the participation of four-year-olds in full-day pre-K programs, particularly when those children may not be ready. She hoped that children such as Tanasia who experienced difficult transitions could instead attend half-day pre-K and spend the rest of the time at home in an enriching and nurturing environment. Here's how I responded:

Thanks for the comment and question. While four-year-olds will, of course, feel attached to the home, I also think there comes a point when adults from the home and school need to facilitate the child's transition to school. For some children, a slower transition involving half-day pre-K is or at least seems more fitting. As a full-day pre-K teacher, I see the benefit of a full day in terms of all of the different kinds of learning we can include (whole group, small group, meal times) to support social and academic growth. As a teacher in the inner city, I also face the reality of households in which all adults need to work full-time. Thus, for both practical and financial reasons and for the social and academic growth of my students, I favor full-day programs.

Abigail Wentworth, a Teach For America corps member who taught half-day kindergarten in Los Angeles responded:

> I teach half-day kindergarten in a low-income community, and I wish that I could teach my students all day. Despite timesaving routines and procedures, multiple teachers in the room, extensive planning, and a lot of hard work, I always feel that my students are being short-changed. Many of the students enter kindergarten with no formal school experience, limited social interaction, and limited experience with books and literacy. My half-day program simply does not leave us with enough time to play catch-up, and I think that the students would really benefit from additional time in school.

JANUARY 19

Which Comes First, the Assessment or the Children?

"Ms. Pappas, look, I found the word *calcium* on my milk carton!" exclaimed Ravon.

"Wow! Great job, Ravon. How do you know it says *calcium?*"

"Because I see the letter 'C' with the other words like *cat* and *car.*"

At this moment, I am thinking three things:
1. I am so proud of Ravon;
2. How fast can I write down exactly what he said on my clipboard, so I can use this exchange as evidence of his growth in early literacy?; and
3. How will I ever balance active teacher-student engagement with anecdotal note-taking if the school district requires me to collect anecdotes on another 50 skills for still another assessment system?

While I appreciate the value of performance-based assessments in helping me target individual student needs, I also sometimes wonder if a drive to make assessment as comprehensive and in-depth as possible comes at the expense of quality teacher-student interaction. I am not sure if state and district policymakers realize what their mandates look like on a day-to-day basis at the school level.

In my school, we now have four types of assessment, soon to be joined by a fifth:

1. The Early Learning Assessment System (ELAS)—a state-mandated performance-based literacy assessment charting student growth in six areas. This is reported three times per year.
2. A district-mandated checklist, charting growth in the areas of social-emotional, gross motor, and fine motor development. This is recorded twice per year.
3. A district-mandated beginning-of-the-year Brigance Screening, used mainly to identify any developmental delays.
4. Math checklists from the district-mandated math curriculum, charting growth in various skill areas. This is recorded three times per year (recommended but not required).

Recently, the pre-K teachers in the district had a workshop that covered a comprehensive anecdotal note-based assessment, which covers 50 skills and is recorded three times per year. I personally like this anecdotal-based assessment, and hope the district will replace other assessments with it. All signs, however, suggest the district will make it supplemental and, therefore, probably more cumbersome than helpful, despite its potential to identify a wide range of student needs.

When this entry first appeared on the Pre-K Now blog, a pre-K teacher at my school who ran early childhood programs in community-based organizations responded with her own comments about the value and challenges of assessments in pre-K:

> I also work in an inner-city district in a pre-K classroom. There is real value in assessing the students. It helps prove the importance of what and how children learn. The problem is that we are told to keep adding different assessments that often overlap. They never just replace or discard an assessment.

FEBRUARY 12

To Teach or to Assess? Is That Really the Question?

David pulled a toy car back and forth. As he released the car he said, "Look, Tyrique! The car going down the road fast. We're gonna have a race."

As I heard David refer to cars and racing, my ears perked up. I had just completed small-group time and was preparing to circulate through our classroom's centers to collect anecdotal observations that show the children's progress, as well as find some great teachable moments. We were exploring transportation, and David was incorporating ideas from class discussions and "read alouds" into his play. While I often have to refer to my individualized student action plans (see sample on page 185) to remember the specific target areas for each child, David has struggled to develop his listening skills for some time, so I knew instantly that it was a breakthrough moment.

Last year, when I first started using the anecdotal note-based assessment system, I typically spent the first couple of weeks of each collection period working with children using their individual plans, rather than recording anecdotes. As I became more comfortable with anecdotal note-based assessments and familiar with my students' needs, my approach has become less compartmentalized. I can now simultaneously assess progress and work with children on other skill areas. I responded to David with questions leading to an informal one-on-one lesson on print awareness and vocabulary.

I said to David, "Great, David, how can we make it go faster? Is there something we can use?"

"Uhh, I don't know."

"What if we used a ramp? Do you know where it is?"

David shrugged his shoulder and said "No."

"You know what; I sometimes forget where it is too. Is there something we could put on the ramp so we know it is a ramp?"

"I don't know."

"Well, (pointing to hat rack) how do you know the hats go here?"

David swept his finger from left to right over the label for hats and said, "Because it says *hats*. Hats, hats, /h/, /h/hats. I see the letter H!"

"So what could we do for the ramp?"

David grabbed a piece of paper and a marker and said, "We could write it."

"Great idea! What should we write for ramp?"

David wrote the letter "R" and said "/rr/R! Like Ravon!"

The next day, David came to me briefly after entering the Blocks Center and, with a strong sense of urgency in his tone asked, "Ms. Pappas, where's the ramp for the cars? I want to make them go fast." The other pre-K teacher unfortunately needed to borrow the ramp, but David was able to use his memory to construct his own ramp using flat boards.

As I prepared for parent-teacher conferences, I noticed dozens of other instances like this one, where a more efficient and dynamic exchange between teaching and assessing has resulted in more substantial student progress. That is not to say that the state or district should inundate teachers with more assessments to maximize teacher quality. There is a tipping point. The question I often hear at teacher workshops—"When am I going to have a chance to teach with all these anecdotal assessments?"—presents a false dichotomy between the two.

When this entry first appeared on the Pre-K Now blog, its reference to the individualized action plans prompted Cheryl Steighner, a first-

year pre-K teacher to ask if I would share the concrete tool.

As a first-year pre-K teacher, I find your blog incredibly helpful. I teach in a similar environment and can relate to several of your posts. I was wondering if you had a sample of your individual action plan you would be willing to share. Also, how do you keep track of your anecdotal notes? I have seen so many different examples, so I am curious.

Thanks so much! Keep writing!

My Response

I use a clipboard for my anecdotal notes. Each student has a sheet of labels I keep on the board. I put tabs on each label with each student's initials so I can just flip to the sheet of labels for the student with whom I am interacting. I then transfer the labels onto anecdotal record sheets provided by my district. (**Note:** A copy of the individual action plan I used is available on page 185 of this book.)

FEBRUARY 14

The Saving Grace of Effective Transitions

Like any good professional educator, I spent hours and hours designing lesson plans. In pre-K, it is especially important that lessons excite and draw on the children's interests. My planning was not complete until I also determined how to transition my children from one lesson activity to the next.

Why are transitions so important in pre-K? Well, take an example from my first year of pre-K teaching. On a typical morning, my students read independently after breakfast, and when that less structured activity ended, I struggled to motivate the class to clean up and focus for the more structured whole-group circle time that followed. I noticed that I spent, on average, 10–15 minutes transitioning the children between the two activities—precious minutes that could have been instructional time.

I reflected on how to minimize time lost to off-task behavior and learned that simple songs and rewards kept the children engaged and attentive as they put away their books or play materials and prepared for the next lesson. Ms.

Morrison taught me a number of chants and songs that we use, including:
- "Read, read, read a book, we are getting smart" (to the tune of "Row, Row, Row, Your Boat")
- "Clean up, clean up, everybody everywhere, clean up, clean up, everybody do your share."
- "Clap, clap, clap, snap, snap, snap, now it's time to take a nap."

I also began providing incentives such as short "dance parties," a fruit we hadn't yet tried, or a visit from a child's family member in return for the class consistently getting ready and focused before I could count down from 10–0. Before long, my class was able to clean up and be ready for our morning meeting in less than one minute. Reclaiming those 10 minutes each day for the entire year adds up to 1,800 minutes of instructional time. Think of what you could teach in 1,800 minutes! And that is just one transition time among eight or nine in a given day.

Time saved is just one benefit of an effective transition. When four-year-olds are standing around while their teacher scrambles to move to the next part of the day, they are apt to fill that vacuum with undesirable behavior. By laying out behavioral expectations at all times, including transitions, and designing transitions that meet students' developmental needs for plenty of movement and singing, transitions help curb those undesirable behaviors. For instance, Ravon, who swung his arms and legs aggressively in the beginning of the year, is far less likely to engage in such behavior now because he knows what kind of behavior I expect of him at all times.

Transitions can also reinforce the concepts and skills we learned throughout the day. As in the examples above, we used counting skills to get ready for circle time and rhyming skills to get ready for nap time and to clean up. Instead of just saying "line up," we lined up in a pattern. Individually, the songs and counting just seem like normal pre-K classroom sounds, but, together, they ensure that the children and I make the most out of each day.

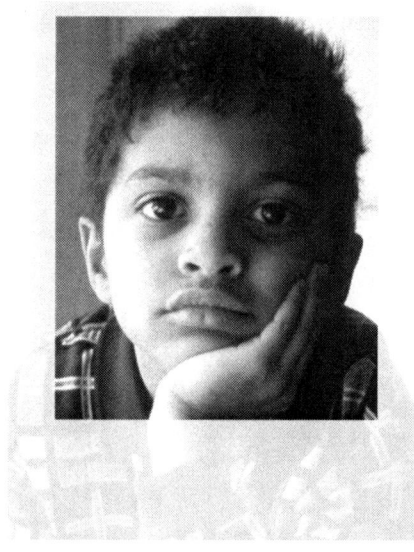

FEBRUARY 25

Dealing with the "F" Word

No matter how many times I tell my kids, "We cannot always do everything we planned; sometimes we have to be flexible," I still feel frustrated when I have to stop a lesson before I intended or change things in the middle of a lesson.

This time it was Friday afternoon and we were just getting into a comparative discussion of Anne Rockwell's *Big Wheels and Cars,* when unexpected visitors arrived: a repair team sent to fix a leak in our radiator. To be honest, when I discovered the leak on Monday, I vacillated between reporting it or just hoping it would go away ... no, not because I want to teach my students about the wonders of flooding or potential gas explosions (though experiential learning would be developmentally appropriate). Rather, I dreaded the prospect of abruptly relocating materials and my students to the auditorium when it came time to fixing it.

Well, it happened. Despite an inner desire to scream out of frustration, as the class' leader I had to redirect my students' attention and moods calmly and quickly. We grabbed some toys, a bin of books, and some map floor mats for continuing our exploration of transportation. We then lined up and headed to the auditorium. The students became so focused on our new mission that we even received a compliment from a fourth-grade teacher who remarked that she has trouble getting her students to behave in such a quiet and organized manner. We finished the literary discussion and then set up informal centers. We also took full advantage of the stage to practice public speaking and rehearse for our future American Idol auditions or Grammy-night performances. Step aside, Beyonce and Justin!

What happened with the leak? Well, at the end of the day, it was not fixed, and we may have to move somewhere else for a few days or the whole week. The uncertainty means the need for more flexibility. There, I said it again. Regardless of my frustration with the situation, I will have to be flexibile because I cannot control the leak, or how long it will take to repair it. All I can do is maximize the constructive learning time with my students.

On Monday morning, I found the furniture still relocated—nothing had been done over the weekend. I organized various centers and whole group materials that my students, Ms. Morrison, and I could transport easily into the library.

The final call that we needed to move came in the middle of our morning meeting. Despite my frustration at having to leave during our attendance routine, I remembered the need to be flexibile and quickly pulled out a rubber band to guide my students. We discussed the need to stretch a little—essentially to "be the rubber band." It turns out my students are incredibly elastic, maybe beyond "rubber-band elastic," even "bungee-cord elastic." They adapted quickly, made creative and print-rich Valentines for family and friends, explored patterns with shapes, sorted "shiny" and "not shiny" coins, and created a backdrop of train tracks for our Dramatic Play Area, just to name a few of the options available.

And the radiator? Unfortunately, they did not finish fixing it. In fact, for whatever reason, they seemed to stop working on it shortly after they arrived. It is now Thursday evening, and we are still unsure when the radiator will be fixed. The saga continues....

When this entry first appeared on the Pre-K Now blog, Kathleen O'Pray contributed her take on the importance of children learning in a safe and predictable environment:

> While I agree it is important for us to be flexible, it is also important for the students to have the security and consistency of having their classroom fixed in a timely

manner. This highlights the need to have communities realize the importance of maintaining the schools their children attend. Communities should be able to take pride in the appearance and safety of their school. After all, who would choose to work for a run-down business?

MARCH 7

Tackling the Digital Divide

"Google it," "blogosphere," "download it"—if you are familiar with these phrases, chances are you use technology on a regular basis, and know many other people who have a similar knowledge base. Contrast this to the children in low-income communities who have little if any access to technology at home. When trying to close school-readiness and achievement gaps, the impact of the "digital divide" cannot be overlooked.

I consider technological awareness—just like math, literacy, and social readiness—one of my main priorities as a pre-K teacher. Children also need to understand the function of the Internet and email because of the vital role these tools play in communication, education, and jobs in our society.

We are fortunate to have two computers in my room, which children can use to play educational games and explore basic applications like Microsoft Paint. I set up the activities before choice time each day and introduce them during our tour of the centers in the beginning of the week. The children can then choose to use the computers during choice time, alone or in pairs. I also set up an email account for the class and invited family and friends to send interesting stories, photos, and questions. We respond as a class using the large "Smart Board" projection screen in our school's Computer Lab. Last year, my friend Alex sent pictures of llamas from his trip to Peru, and the students contemplated and answered his question about whether they would want to ride a llama or a horse.

This week we learned about researching online. The students came up with questions about animals and brought them to the Computer Lab along with clipboards and pencils. I searched online for answers to their questions while the students took notes using drawings and words.

Our first question was, "What do zebras eat?" I walked the students through the process of using a search engine, and we discovered that zebras eat grass. The students drew the zebra they saw in the photograph and labeled it. One astute note taker, Ali, raised her hand when I scrolled down to the picture past the words and said, "Wait, Ms. Pappas, go back so I can write *zebra.*"

We also explored bear and bat caves, lions, and dogs. The only disappointing part was when we had to leave, so many of the children wanted to look up additional animals. We will have to wait until next week because most of my students do not have access to technology at home.

MARCH 20

Whose Curriculum Is it Anyway?

Curricula decisions in pre-K affect everything from what students learn to how they learn it. While many early childhood curricula promote developmentally appropriate practices, I believe some—particularly the scripted programs—fail to capitalize on the "teachable moments" that occur every day in the classroom. As one blog reader recently commented, a scripted program "doesn't really get to high-level thinking questions, doesn't address the needs of kids in individual classrooms."

A highly passionate and organized teacher can make the most of any curriculum. Still, the ability of teachers to adjust specific curricula often depends on a school's or center's relationships with the district, company, or other organization it reports to, as well as teachers' relationships with their direct supervisors.

I recognized the strengths and limitations of the scripted curriculum my district used and engaged my students in meaningful dialogue that came out of our own discussions, regardless of the exact questions the curriculum manual prescribed. This worked largely because my supervisors did not micromanage my classroom (not a benefit every teacher has).

When it came to handling a curriculum switch, my district notified the pre-K teachers of the new curriculum during a summer workshop about a month and a half before school started. Prior to the announcement, we knew only that district officials in the Office of Early Childhood had been vacillating between a few curricula. We were never informed of possible opportunities to voice our opinions based on classroom experiences. Clearly, teacher input and evaluation were not top priorities.

I think my experience with curriculum decisions is hardly unique and begs an important question, "What role, if any, should teachers play in choosing a curriculum?"

When this entry first appeared on the Pre-K Now blog, it prompted John Holland, a Head Start teacher in Richmond, Virginia who writes his own blog at www.circle-time.blogspot.com, *to comment on the development of his own thinking and participation in ECE advocacy work. We proceeded to engage in a dialogue about the challenges and prospects of teachers gaining a voice among policymakers.*

Hi, Sophia,

The two sentences I wanted to respond to are: "We were never informed of possible opportunities to voice our opinions based on classroom experiences. Clearly, teacher input and evaluation were not top priorities." I appreciate your perspective and shared it for a long time. Recently, I have changed my position. I believe it is our responsibility to carve a voice out of the din for decisions that regard educating young children.

John

My Response

Thanks for the note. I read the excerpt from your essay and agree with your insights on the need for teachers to take more initiative in education reform. I actually did ask my resource teacher at one point about voicing our opinions on the curriculum issue. She said there were committees we could have signed up for the year before when I was not yet in the classroom. She also said she and the other resource teachers try to have a say, but are shut out. This does not excuse my lack of effort to challenge her and the decisions of the district office, but it does reveal a somewhat undemocratic culture among the decision-makers in this instance. I also think that while teachers should organize to have their voices heard, sometimes it is difficult to meet the needs of our students while also taking on those leadership roles.

Lastly, I think more individuals who have left the classroom should consider taking on full-time roles in policymaking. The insights gained, as you have noted, are incredibly valuable.

John's Response

I apologize for just getting back to your response. I have been busy preparing a speech for the Virginia Department of Education. I am taking a very informative class from the President of the Virginia Board of Education. He is a very dynamic person, but most importantly, he has learned and begun to teach me how administrators make decisions in education. One way to start having a voice in affecting the direction of education programs is by contacting state-and district-level members of your boards of education. Before I contacted my local and state board members, my impression was that they were strictly politically minded people, and I thought they were more interested in protecting their careers and accumulating power and authority than they were in taking risks to effect change. After getting to know some of these people, I have begun to see that many policymakers really do value teachers (though some do not) and that many would be happy to hear from us. These policymakers want to help, and are interested in finding good causes for which to advocate.

My Response

It is great to hear that you have found politicians willing to listen to educators and factor their ideas into policy decisions. Such partnerships are crucial for generating real change. There will obviously always be some policymakers and educators with questionable motives, but I agree that if we can build relationships with well-intentioned folks on both sides, we can start to reform the system for the better. I personally plan to move on from the classroom at some point to study public policy and then go into politics.

When this entry first appeared on the Pre-K Now blog, I also heard from a teacher who expressed a strong aversion to scripted programs, given their inability to meet individual students' needs. She wanted advice on how teachers at her school might bring in unscripted curricula. I could not offer suggestions because the ECE leadership in my district made the change. Yet her comments raised interesting questions regarding influence and authority in early childhood education:
1. *Who should make curricula decisions including both the particular programs districts*

and schools use and the pool of programs from which to choose?

2. *What role should teachers, administrators, parents, and even students play in this decision-making process and evaluation of programs after they have been implemented? A four-year-old would not sit in on a district or state-run committee, but data from children's progress and level of engagement with curricula would, in effect, give them a voice at the table.*

Several months after this dialogue, I discussed these issues with a class on public policy at my alma mater. I explained to the students who inquired about curricula decisions how my district decided to adopt one unscripted curriculum for all pre-K teachers to establish a more streamlined and effective system of professional development. The professor recognized the possible increased efficiency of this approach, but also argued that such top-down decision making undermines the professionalism of teachers by relinquishing their control over the instructional choices in their classroom. I responded by noting that while some teachers I met wished they had more freedom to make those kinds of choices, several others sought more, not less, structure and guidance from the district.

MARCH 28

Not All Assessments Are Created Equal

The debate over Head Start's National Reporting System got me thinking about the challenges of assessing what three-and four-year-olds know and what they have learned from their pre-K teachers.

Not being a Head Start teacher myself, I have never administered the NRS. I am required, however, to use a screening assessment on all my students at the beginning of each school year to identify any potential developmental delays. While some of the parts of the screening process are helpful (such as following two-and three-step directions; fine motor and gross motor evaluations), many of the questions seem to measure a child's exposure to certain words and objects rather than development. For example, one portion of the screening asks the child to identify a picture of a tractor. I personally fail to see how the inability of a four-year-old from the inner city to identify a tractor indicates any sort of developmental delay. The screening also requires children to identify several body parts including the jaw and ankle, a stretch for any four-year-old in my opinion.

I think my ideal pre-K assessment tool would break down the four areas of child development (social/emotional; physical; cognitive; and language) and be able to measure each of those components, regardless of a child's background. Unlike our current screening process, such an assessment may have to be partially or entirely anecdotal-based, because children may not reveal the full extent of their problem-solving or language skills in one or two one-to-one interactions at the start of the year. A teacher can, however, observe a child within the context of play, looking at the materials and areas the child chooses.

There are other assessment systems that are more thoroughly anecdotal-based, and that use a continuum of child development to assess all four areas of development. In my opinion, these strategies provide the most comprehensive assessment opportunity. While such assessments can be quite helpful in providing information about your students, the assessments are not necessarily the most accessible kinds of data for kindergarten teachers to use the following year, so I do think the more traditional assessments (letter identification, book-handling checklist) have a role to play. Moreover, while these assessments often include rubric-like structures with indicators for each objective, they can also be subjective as teachers interpret student behaviors in a wide range of contexts to determine where they fall on a continuum for each skill.

The interesting thing about all of this is that, while I have reservations about our current assessment program, nobody from the district has ever discussed my students' test scores with me either as a reflection of my effectiveness as a teacher or my students' readiness for kindergarten. We have adopted a state-mandated, anecdotal note-based assessment system that some district resource teachers say the state will use to inform their decisions about funding. Regardless, in the three years that I have been in the classroom, all the assessments sent "downtown" just seem like mounds of paperwork being thrown into an abyss, never to be referred to again. I certainly use my assessments both to tailor my instruction to meet student needs and to reflect on my own growth as a teacher. Yet the only feedback I receive from administrators and district personnel focuses on their in-class observations of my classroom teaching and my promptness in handing in paperwork.

I am not sure that the federal and New Jersey governments have pre-K assessment and accountability down pat. I think policymakers need to collaborate with educators as they rethink all assessments. In the end, teacher quality directly affects student outcomes, and teachers should be held accountable for their students' growth. In order to create an effective program of collaboration and accountability, we need to agree on what things are important to measure and how we should measure them. Effective programs, like pre-K, deserve effective assessment, not just assessment for assessment's sake.

APRIL 17

Tax Tips: IRS Says I Am Not an Eligible Educator

Tax season can be, well, taxing. At least educators can rest assured that the federal government will honor their professional commitment by offering a deduction for some of their own financial investments in their classrooms. That is, unless you teach pre-K. As I found out this year, only K–12 educators are eligible for such a deduction.

Pre-K teachers, like our counterparts in K–12, often use money from our own pockets to purchase classroom materials that benefit the children we teach. Here is one simple thing federal policymakers could do to make early childhood educators feel as valued as other teachers: amend the tax code to make us eligible for the educator expense deduction. Happy Tax Day!

APRIL 19

Praise with a Purpose

Effective praise is a crucial element of a strong pre-K classroom. As any early childhood educator or family member will tell you, young learners constantly seek validation from adults. In response, I try to provide support for my students' achievements to instill in them the self-confidence they need to take risks as learners and to remain highly motivated. That said, "being positive" does not necessarily benefit young learners.

Consider how we, as adults, become better at something professionally. If a boss or colleague simply says, "Good work," we cannot be sure what was good and how we can continue improving in the future. If the coworker is specific and genuine, however, we feel not only confident in our abilities but also empowered to produce "good work" later on.

This principle holds when working with young children. A student might approach me with a piece of artwork, for example, and I may feel inclined to comment on how beautiful it is. The student, however, walks away from that exchange with no understanding of the strengths he exhibited or areas he could work on. While it takes more thought and effort, I aim to engage each child in a dialogue with comments and questions such as, "Interesting, I like the way you used three different colors on the top part of your design. Why did you use three colors on top and one color on the bottom? Tell me about the design. What could you add to the horse?" Through dialogue, I can focus the child on specific aspects of the work and invite him to reflect on his work.

It is amazing to see and hear such a reflection actually take place. I often hear my students think aloud and address the points we brought up in earlier discussions. For example, Ravon recently noted, "Oh, the cow has eyes to see just like me," before he added eyes to his drawing. Tyrone now engages in a dialogue with himself as he writes independently. While labeling his cat mask during small group recently, he asked himself, "How do you spell cat?" and then responded, "You need to stretch it out, c–aaaaaaaaaaa–ttt" as he pulled his hands apart the way we had discussed in a one-on-one guided writing session.

In a given day, between small group and whole group lessons, anecdotal note-taking and snack time, providing specific and authentic praise that invites further reflection seems difficult. Nevertheless, praise with a purpose is so effective and rewarding that I encourage everyone around young children, in or out of the classroom, to do it.

When this entry first appeared on the Pre-K Now blog, this piece attracted the attention of John Holland, who became a frequent blog visitor and commenter and contributed some great ideas from his own classroom:

> Another great post, Sophia! One of my favorite strategies is to reflect what a student says. I usually start with the statement, "Tell me about your picture." When Daniel says, "I drew my daddy," by simply saying, "Your daddy?" it often elicits an entire story from a child. How do you handle students who aren't trying or pushing themselves though? The ones you think can do better?

My Response

Thanks for the comment and question. I also use the "tell me about your..." technique in a variety of settings (for example, in blocks, "tell me about your construction or building," or in Sand or Dramatic Play "tell me about what you're doing" to begin a dialogue).

In terms of motivating students, I occasionally do the activity along with them if I notice they are not putting much effort into it. I model thinking aloud about my picture as well as what to do when I am stuck. I then invite the child to help me (for example, "I am going to draw a picture too. Let's see, we sang that fun song about recycling. I think I will draw myself throwing paper in the recycling bin. But how do I get started? Which part of me do I draw first? Should I just give up, cry, or keep going?"). It is usually at this point that the child steps in to help. I make sure I thank the child for helping me, for example, saying, "That was fun, now let's work on your drawing!"

I also try to target their interests. If I know a child likes cars, I may try to incorporate cars in my questioning. For example, I could ask "What else could you draw? I remember you talking about cars at lunch. Would you like to put a car in your drawing?"

I have also found that even the children having a bad day respond well to a burst of silliness. In the car situation, I might say, "Gee, if we are going to draw a car we better make it flying in the sky with a pig on top. What? That is not right. Well, can you show me what a car would really look like?"

Lastly, we have an "easy" button for times when we think something is difficult, but then work through it. I may show other children pressing the easy button when they are done to motivate the other child.

MAY 3

A Sign of Equality for Pre-K Teachers

In the immortal words of Homer Simpson: "Woo-hoo!" This week is Educator Appreciation Week at my local bookstore. Lucky for teachers, this store (and many bookstores), unlike the IRS, includes pre-K teachers in its special offerings: 25% off classroom and personal purchases. To all pre-K educators out there, bring a pay stub or your union card to prove you are a teacher.

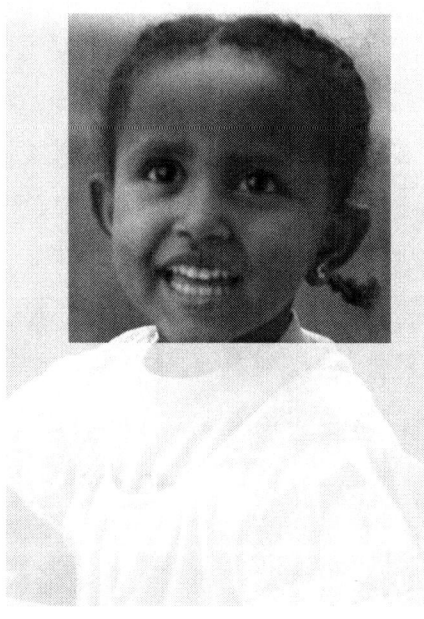

MAY 21

Snowed Under

No, I am not digging out from an anomalous May snowstorm, but I do feel quite overwhelmed by end-of-the-year paperwork. Like other teachers, I have mostly assessments and annual school-wide progress forms to complete this time of year. My pre-K program has additional sets of assessments handed down by the district and the state.

The state mandates the use of ELAS, a performance-based assessment system focusing on six language arts/literacy expectations. Normally, I would not voice any concerns about ELAS. Despite the tedious paperwork involved, it has been very helpful as a tool for targeting the strengths and weaknesses of my students. That said, I do have a concern: the collection period for ELAS ends in June, but my support person from the Office of Early Childhood has insisted we hand in the paperwork nearly a month earlier. Why? My guess is because other pre-K sites have been delinquent in handing in paperwork on time in the past.

The problems with this creative revision of the ELAS timetable are threefold:

1. This time of year, many pre-K students start to demonstrate remarkable academic progress, especially those who entered pre-K younger than the other students. If we stop collecting anecdotes and work samples from those children in mid-May (to ensure we can finish the paperwork before Memorial Day), we may fail to capture this growth and, thereby, provide the state, our schools, and families with inaccurate results.
2. We are also responsible for a completing a social skills checklist and the district's experimental assessment forms (requiring the collection of anecdotes covering more than 30 expectations) in the same period. Now, I am all for an Amazing Race-style challenge for teachers to balance three assessment systems simultaneously, while also instructing students. That said, if we are really in early childhood for the children and not just to satisfy the sadistic cravings of paperwork-hungry bureaucrats, we should think realistically about how demands on teachers affect their ability to perform in the classroom.
3. I have always handed in paperwork on time along with additional individualized action plans (see sample on page 185) for my students. If the folks at the Office of

Early Childhood were as organized and well managed as they should be, they would put additional pressure only on those teachers who need it. In a sense, they should differentiate their approach to employees in the same way that they require teachers to differentiate our approach for the varying needs of our students.

Well, I have to go now; this paperwork is not going to fill itself out.

JUNE 12

The Tough Questions

Many of my children, though only four or five years old, have already dealt with difficult situations in their lives, anything from foster care or parental incarceration to homelessness. While these issues can affect a child's perspective and ability to trust others, parental incarceration recently posed a challenge for me. The negative experiences with the police that some children may bring into the classroom can make it particularly tricky to present law enforcement in a positive light.

Last week, we held Career Day at our school. To prepare, we discussed possible jobs such as doctor, police officer, and dancer, and as a class composed a letter welcoming the Career Day participants. During our pre-writing discussion, I asked the students how they felt about Career Day. Tyrone responded, "I feel angry because the police are gonna come and lock everyone up." His comment reminded me of an earlier comment from Ali that also expressed distrust of the police and suggested we physically hurt the police so they "won't do that anymore."

I began to explain the reasons why people might go to jail and emphasized the positive role of police officers in making us safe. I could not help but glance at two of my other students who currently have family members in jail. They did not say anything, but I wondered what might be going on in their heads. "Is my mommy wrong? Is she making people unsafe? Is it a good thing that the police took my daddy away from me? If the police are good, is my daddy bad?"

As I considered these thoughts, I began to backpedal. I talked briefly about people making mistakes and responded to a question about everyone going to jail "for life" by stressing that many times people in jail get to leave and be with their families again. I then wondered, for Tyrique—who is just developing a sense of time and who will be 15 when his mother gets out—what is the real difference between a life apart from his mother and 10 years spent apart from her during his crucial childhood years?

I am aware of the sensitivity of these issues and the larger reality of mixed attitudes toward the police in inner city neighborhoods. What is not clear is how to deal with them in a way that will both preserve strong ties between children and their families and define the police as a source of protection for the people in those neighborhoods. Stories of gang violence permeate the evening news; and it would be difficult to find a social science article about crime in the United States that did not include statistics on incarceration among young people, particularly males, in urban areas. Too often, the children involved in those situations and their relationships with incarcerated family members are excluded from the narrative. Just like anything else in a child's life, their firsthand experience with these issues can shape their attitudes later on. I do not have a list of concrete strategies, but schools should devise an approach that reflects these tensions and the realities of student-family relations. Not all children in the inner city have family members in prison, and not all children and families who do handle it in the same way. Many children, at least from my experience, have strong connections to family members serving time, and family members returning from incarceration often take active and positive roles in their children's lives, as I saw with a few of my students' fathers. Moreover, the family members still at home can support the school's effort to address the issue.

The world of prisons technically exists outside of the school, but the children affected by prison come to class every day with the right to encounter teachers who take responsibility for increasing their life prospects—whether that means differentiating their approach to counting or helping students grapple with complicated issues that could ultimately influence their ability to be safe and productive citizens.

JUNE 13

The Frightening Prospect of Self-Fulfilling Prophesies

Earlier in the year, I talked to a kindergarten teacher about how his class was doing this year. He lamented the fact that many of his students did not know how to read and write and said that, "Luckily, some of them come from good families, so they should do okay." I chose to refrain from an outright confrontation and instead just focus on the growth of my own students. This teacher's remarks, however, struck me as disturbing on a number of levels. I started to wonder what effect a lifetime of authority figures sending the message to certain children that they are simply not fit to realize their own potential would have on those children's attitudes towards themselves and others and their overall life trajectory.

I remember an assembly where members of the Newark Police Department and a prisoner who had been involved with gangs talked to the students. The police officer said that their gang-violence education campaign did not include an explicit instruction not to join gangs, but just information on what has happened to individuals involved with gangs. One of my colleagues responded by telling her class straightforwardly, "Don't join gangs—period!" While this direction is positive, the statement, in and of itself, narrowly defines the responsibilities of educators. Gangs can provide a sense of belonging and empowerment. They say to a child who has never felt successful or valued in school, "We promise you loyalty and the chance to feel validated by your efforts." To grow as learners and members of a group, children need to trust that if they take risks and fail, someone will be there to support them with positive reinforcement and varied instructional approaches that meet their needs. If, however, teachers respond to student weaknesses by embarrassing them or failing to differentiate for students of varying abilities and learning styles, those students may never develop critical skills and confidence in their ability to flourish within the context of school. Teachers who tell their students not to join gangs after an assembly in October, but then spend the rest of the year inadequately meeting the academic and social needs of their students, risk undermining their anti-gang crusade and, in effect, push their students further away from a productive, safe, and lawful life path.

I certainly take for granted the fact that I come from a privileged background. In fact, trust in one's own abilities and confidence that society will reward one's efforts with opportunities and just treatment is certainly not a universal or inevitable part of a person's psyche. Even if a child receives that kind of positive reinforcement before entering school, teachers who don't believe in students can squash that kind optimism and diminish a child's life prospects. We do not typically assign that level of power to teachers, but, for many students, teachers represent the attitudes and opinions of society at-large.

I do not mean to diminish the influence other adults have on a child's life. Nor do I mean to suggest that all of the teachers at my school exhibited judgmental attitudes that would negatively affect students' self-perceptions. Ultimately, the solution to gang violence and other negative trends in inner cities must entail coordinated efforts with a wide range of community members who unite around a shared purpose. True collective responsibility (and not the kind that becomes diffused to the point where nobody is really held accountable) requires each actor to acknowledge his or her role and to positively maximize his or her sphere of influence. As a teacher, I can identify specific ways educators can either promote or discourage participation in gangs. This process should not perpetuate the blame game that seems to paralyze reform. Rather, it should empower teachers to use their position in the classroom as an opportunity to expand the life prospects of their students. This kind of mindset means the following to me, as a pre-K teacher: When students enter my classroom as four-year-olds, I do not see that first day as the chance to welcome students just to my classroom. I am introducing these students to the world outside of their homes—the society in which they will operate as students, employees, and citizens for the rest of their lives. This broader view of my role in the students' lives means I have a greater opportunity to have a positive impact. I must provide students with a sense of belonging. I do this in the following ways:

- Putting each student's name on an individual cubby the moment each student walks in the door;
- Assigning each student a classroom job in the first week after a written (or drawn) and oral interview;
- Validating my students' interests by engaging in conversations about their families and favorite activities and using those insights to inform my instructional choices;

- Treating my students with dignity and respect in the way that I respond to positive and negative behavioral choices they make (this includes offering authentic praise and logical consequences); and
- Crafting lessons in whole group, small group, centers, and one-on-one interactions that reflect my students' needs in all developmental domains, personalities, and interests.

While these strategies serve a practical purpose in the everyday functioning of my classroom, my commitment to executing them effectively and consistently derives in large part from my belief of the positive, long-term impact they can have on my students' achievements.

JUNE 22

A Fair Shot

As my children prepare for pre-K graduation and the move to kindergarten, I cannot help but wonder about their futures. Will Ali become a doctor? Will Awana have the chance to choose between being a ballerina or a doctor? Will Karen's behavior regress and threaten her academic progress?

I have worked to introduce my students to school, making it seem like an exciting and fun place where they can make friends, learn, and be successful. Anecdotal evidence and various forms of assessments suggest that my students have already started to realize their potential and are on the path toward high achievement in school and beyond. The strong attendance of family members at our class events, and their interest in enriching their children's thinking skills over the summer also bode well for my students' academic prospects.

Yet my students still have many years during which their attitudes toward school, themselves, and their peers can change for the worse. Most of them will continue to live in unsafe neighborhoods and struggling school districts. It gives me hope to know that research shows students in inner-city schools who have had high-quality pre-K have a greater rate of success in school and beyond than those who do not attend pre-K programs. I know that my instruction in the classroom and the active support of family members during this critical stage in children's development will have life-long benefits. I also believe innovative changes are occurring in the K–12 system, many of them spearheaded by my fellow Teach For America alums. Still, on an individual level, it is still hard to predict how successfully the children in my class will build on the pre-K foundation they gained this year.

My time in the classroom has been, above all, about providing the kinds of opportunities that all students deserve. The playing field is not level, even for three-and four-year-olds. High-quality pre-K teachers alone cannot ensure that a child will not face educational and societal inequities down the road, but the vibrant and challenging learning environments we provide are the first step toward giving all children an equal chance at success.

From Good to Great: Academic Growth in Pre-K 114

Introduction

I write this introduction in Cambridge, Massachusetts where I am attending the Kennedy School of Government for a master's in Public Policy. I have been blessed with a lifetime of opportunities and privileges including parents who surrounded me with academically enriching materials and activities. My trajectory from a toddler exploring the alphabet to a Harvard graduate student began with a strong foundation of skills and knowledge during each critical stage in my development.

Some of my students entered my classroom with an understanding of basic cognitive and literacy skills, but many did not, and statistics show that the achievement gap present before kindergarten gets wider and more difficult to close after those early elementary years. Highly inviting and supportive environments are important for pre-K, but from my experience, teachers can focus on the growth of their children in foundational skills as well. I did not use "drill-kill" tactics nor did I allow students who entered my room to leave without the foundation they would need to be successful in elementary school and beyond. I seized every moment as a learning opportunity, whether we were on the rug during circle time, in the Dramatic Play Center during center time, or at the tables during meals. I used ongoing assessments to stay on the pulse of each child's needs.

Just as we should not squander the opportunity to identify school as a safe and welcoming place, we should also demonstrate to students that they can succeed as productive learners. Ultimately, they need both to achieve their goals.

DECEMBER 12

Wow!

I definitely had a "wow" moment today with my student Awana. Awana came into our classroom in September with little knowledge and awareness of print, colors, numbers, or shapes. Although Ms. Morrison, my aide, and I have been working closely with Awana, we did not see significant progress until this past week. The great thing about her progress was that it came not just from our direct interactions with Awana, but also from Awana's interactions with other students, her "fellow scholars."

During afternoon choice time, I found Awana writing letters on whiteboards with a small group of her friends. First, I was happy to see Awana using the whiteboard marker from her own kit, since, for the first month or so, she would confuse her name with others and, consequently, use materials from other students' supply kits. Her friends supported her growth in this area by helping her find her supply kit numerous times.

Then, Awana and I had a conversation. I asked her, "What are you writing, Awana?"

"My friends."

"Oh, whose name is this?" I said as I pointed to the letter "S" Awana had written.

"Samar."

"And what about this letter. What is that?" I said, pointing to the letter "A."

"A."

"Whose name starts with the letter 'A'?"

"My name."

"Who else has a name that starts with the letter 'A'?"

"Ali."

As we discussed her writing, some of her friends began to take out notepaper and envelopes. Awana quickly jumped up and said, "I'm going to write a letter." She watched her friends and followed their lead. One of her friends reminded her to put a name on her envelope. They both dropped their letters in the mailbox and moved on to something else.

The placement of children's names all around the room, from cubbies to classroom job charts, to mats, paid off. Moreover, Awana's interactions with her friends generated an excitement for writing. She displayed an interest in writing the letters that represent her friends' names, as well as writing a letter to her mother, which reflected a growing awareness of how to use writing in everyday life.

JANUARY 3

Students as Teachers: An Amazing First Day Back

"Happy New Year!" I exclaimed to each of my students as they walked in today. In the past, this week back after the holiday break often proved somewhat hectic, with many of the children needing some time to get back into the swing of our daily routines. This year's return is shaping up differently. Here are a couple of highlights from the first day back:

- While I planned to review our "talk it out" approach to conflict resolution later in the week, the students independently devised their own scenarios today. As part of our introduction to a three-week exploration of winter, I showed them images of two bears: one fully dressed for winter and the other wearing only a T-shirt. After we passed the images around, I asked the students what they noticed about the two bears. Samar responded imaginatively by saying, "That bear with the jacket hit the other bear with a block." We then began discussing various ways we could respond to such a situation. The students came up with everything from apologizing and telling an adult to getting another block so the two bears could share. We ultimately did talk about and explore winter throughout the day, but the teachable moment involving the bears was particularly valuable because it derived from student interest and demonstrated their deepening understanding of how to solve conflicts.

- After reading the poem "Chicken Soup with Rice" for January, we went to the auditorium, laced up our make-believe skates and tried pretend skating while sipping our own soup. We discussed potential dangers, such as, "wind that could blow leaves in your soup" (Kevin);"rain that could make the soup taste nasty" (Derrell); and, "snow that could make the soup cold" (Sierra). As we skated around the auditorium, we managed to escape a wolf "hiding behind a tree" (Jeffrey), but suddenly a dragon appeared. We just started exploring snow and ice today, so, like any good pre-K teacher with Greek roots, I had to use a bit of the Socratic method. After breaking it down with detailed questions, we figured out that the fire from the dragon would melt the ice, causing us to have to swim back to our classroom instead of ice skate. As Ravon said, "Whew, that was a close one!"

MARCH 22

The Power of Planning

"Your students' growth will be your growth"—wise words from one of my three greatest role models as a teacher, an experienced Teach For America teacher who taught in my district.

Each year, as we begin to discuss signs of spring in the sprouting flowers and leaves outside, I also notice my students' academic growth, particularly in basic literacy skills. As I observe them throughout the day, I see how the individual action plans (see samples on pages 183 and 185) I created and implemented facilitated their development and achievement. The anecdotal notes and work samples in their portfolios provided insights into my students' strengths and weaknesses. I then used that data to develop teaching plans, both for myself and for the students' families to follow. While I started using these plans last year, more practice with anecdotal note-taking and familiarity with analyzing skill deficits using our performance-based assessments strengthened my ability to target and address student needs this year. The success of this valuable teaching tool makes me feel like I have really improved as an instructional leader.

Here are just a few examples of their growth:

- David's anecdotal notes and work samples from the fall revealed the need to work on listening skills (such as incorporating ideas from discussions into play). Consequently, I linked my questions before and during choice time to ideas that we discussed during circle time. I also brought in more topics that seemed to appeal to him, such as transportation and animals. David recently approached me with a toy airplane and his name card. He placed the laminated card flat on the table, slid the airplane across the card, and just before raising the plane in the air exclaimed, "Look, Ms. Pappas, the airplane is about to take off on the runway. It can't just go straight up, it has to go like this," as he rolled the airplane on the flat surface and then had it take off.
- Tyrone's target areas in the fall included relating stories to his own life. I worked on this skill with Tyrone in whole and small group settings, modeling how to connect stories to our own experiences. For example, during a read-aloud of Dr. Seuss' *The Cat in the Hat,* I might relate to the experience of the children sitting at home on a rainy day by saying, "I remember when it

was pouring rain and I couldn't go outside to play tag with my friends. I felt sad." I also designed activities that encouraged the students to compare and contrast characters' lives with their own. Tyrone's recent literary insights include, "I took a long train like the one in the book to New York" and "I went to the zoo too. I saw an elephant."

- In the fall, Fuquan exhibited strong letter-identification skills and was starting to identify beginning sounds in words. From that foundation, he needed to work on making letter-sound connections and using that skill to write words. My plan for him included playing letter-sound sorting games in small group, discussing sounds in words during one-on-one activities like journal time, and singing songs about letter sounds during transition times. Fuquan is now labeling his drawings with the letters that match the pictures. He can also write short sentences, with some adult guidance.

I look forward to using my improved planning skills to make the most of the precious few months left with my students this school year.

MARCH 23

Center Cards and Math/Literacy Enrichment

Teachers can use procedures to teach and reinforce basic skills. Our center card system helped develop students' understanding of foundational math and literacy skills.

Each of the children has a laminated card with the first letter of their names written in red and the rest of their names written in black. At the beginning of choice time, I have two managers (two students in the class) hand out the cards either on their own or by asking their friends for help. In addition to playing several name games and puzzles early on with the students as ways to familiarize them with one another's names and help them recognize their names in print, I focus on a few names a day at the beginning of center time. The students examine them, figure out whose names they are, and then call out names using just the first letter, sound, or rhyming their name using a particular letter (such as Syrone instead of Tyrone). Once I go through all of the names and immerse children in the printed names throughout the day, nearly all of them can identify their own names and some of the names of their peers. This entire process typically takes 2–3 weeks.

The early literacy skills these activities teach:
- Concepts of print—reading from left to right; print carries meaning;
- Letter-sound connections—highlights the first letter and sound of their name, which they hear all the time, and the names of their friends;
- Letter identification;
- Letter sound identification; and
- Rhyming.

Students then choose centers one-by-one with the understanding that given the space in each center only a limited number of students can be in certain centers at a time (for example, the Dramatic Play Center can fit only four people at a time). Each center has a cardboard video box taped to the entrance with the name of the center, the number of smiley faces that correspond to the number of children that can be in that center at a time, and the numeral representing that number. If the box has no smiley faces, there is no limit (for example, the Library). The whole class learns how to count the smiley faces and the cards in each center box to determine if they can enter the center in the beginning of the year. At first, I have to re-teach these skills to individual students, but after a while, other students help and everyone picks up on it. For students who pick up on the skill quickly, you can advance their thinking further by asking questions like, how many more people need to come to this center for it to be full? What are the different ways you can figure out how many people are in a center at a given time? How many people are in the Dramatic Play Center and Blocks Center combined? I see a numeral here, but I do not know what it says. How could I find out?

The early math skills this teaches:
- One-to-one correspondence,
- Counting, and
- Numeral identification.

APRIL 27

Awana's Struggles and Successes

This time of year can be bittersweet, with many students demonstrating remarkable growth and others still struggling with some basic skills. Awana can do both, depending on the day or even the hour.

I recognized her needs early on, and have been working with her intensely in one-on-one sessions, in addition to our small and large group lessons. Awana started making connections in December when she wrote her friends' names in the Writing Center. Awana could recall the formation and order of the letters for most of her friends' names and had developed the fine motor skills needed to write those names. She could not, however, identify the letters or the sounds in those names. This pointed out the importance of Awana's friends as a reference point for her further growth in literacy. Similarly, it illustrated the importance of building on that foundation with instruction that helps Awana make connections between words, letters, and letter sounds. If Awana chose to draw and write about dogs, we thought about the sound in the word dog. Awana thought about the dog, listened for the /d/ sound, said, "like in David's name," and then wrote the letter D.

As I used this plan in my work with Awana, I noticed that her friends' names were not the only useful resource. The transition chants that focused on letters (and which we sing every day) also helped Awana make connections during choice time and in small group. For example, one day we might move from the daily schedule routine to a letter exploration activity by chanting, "Big 'L'! Little 'l'! What begins with 'L'? Lunch, lunch, /l//l/Lunch." Recently, as a part of our study of the environment, the class wrote a letter to the mayor about the littering problem in Newark. To help us get writing, I thought aloud for the children, saying, "Hmm ... litter, what sounds do you hear in the word *litter.*" Before I could "struggle" with the difficult challenge, Awana's hand shot up. She responded, "/l/, Big 'L'! Little 'l'! What begins with 'L'? Lunch, lunch, /l//l/Lunch." She then proudly came up to the board to add the letter "L."

Although Awana has made great strides in developing her literacy skills, she does not always retain the information she learns. Many times during the day, Awana responds to certain activities by shrugging her shoulders and remaining silent or just calling out random letters (and sometimes even numbers). I realize some of the inconsistency may be developmental, but I have never seen such dramatic differences in the same student within the same day.

There is also Awana's mother. Out of all my students, Awana receives the least amount of support from home. In June, I hope to send each of the students in my class home with a toolkit filled with games their families can play with them over the summer, helping them retain the skills they gained through the year. Awana will need this support the most, but given the difficulty her mother has had in keeping appointments with me this year, I fear that Awana will not get this support, and that these hard-won skills may fade.

MAY 1

Ready for Take-Off: David's Story

Four months ago, David's mother remarked that she wants her son to go "sky high in life." Now, as he begins to transition to kindergarten, David shows tremendous social and academic progress. His story shows how high-quality pre-K supports multiple facets of childhood development.

Socially, David adjusted quickly to our rules and routines back in the fall, but he tended to avoid playing with others and participating actively in large group activities. He was reluctant to sing along with the group or respond during a read-aloud. Rather than playing with his friends in crowded areas such as the Blocks and Sand Center, David preferred playing with dinosaurs by himself in the Discovery Center. The challenge was to have him go beyond just following all the rules as an individual, and to begin collaborating more with his peers and participating during whole group lessons.

To help his growth in this area, I encouraged David and his classmates to support their friends by cheering them on with individualized chants. For example, the students would use chants like the following to encourage one another: "There is a friend who's in our class, and David is his name-o. D-a-v-id, D-a-v-i-d, D-a-v-i-d, and David is his name-o!" I also used stories and puppet role-plays to facilitate discussions about how we can help each other solve problems. For instance, if our friends are struggling with a task, we can help them remember *The Little Engine that Could* by saying, "I think you can, I think you can."

David soon started having breakthrough moments. He expressed pride in himself by informing his mother of his "purple" status (this status is part of a color-based reward system I use) the moment she picked him up. The next day, David would let me know how proud his dad was when he told his father about his purple status. David also started contributing more on the rug. Just this week, David got to purple for his active participation throughout the day. In terms of playing with others, David often travels between play areas with friends, most notably last week when he and Tyrique together made newspaper hats in the Art Center and then drew a pirate adventure on the chalk board in the Writing Center.

Academically, David came to pre-K knowing some letters, and starting to be able to write his name, but he had difficulty counting, making connections between letters and their sounds, and with forming letters. I soon made him the snack manager, which required David to count his friends every day. Ms. Morrison and I worked with him in small group, challenging him to work with name puzzles and pointing out print and letter sounds to him at every opportunity. His mother was quick to invest herself in David's efforts, and his father soon followed. They helped him learn how to write the sight words he would learn in school. They helped him label the pictures he drew, using the beginning letters of each object and person. They challenged David to count in a variety of everyday routines (such as counting the number of dishes needed for dinner or the number of shirts in the laundry). Also, as they noted in their New Year's Resolution, David's parents read with him every night. His father remarked at one of our conferences that David was so excited about books, he would often stop his father during stories to make comments. I kept David's parents updated on specific strengths, weaknesses, and ways they could help David continue to learn and grow. From the progress David was making in his writing skills and from hearing him explore letter sounds, I could tell that his parents were using the strategies at home with great success.

David can now write short sentences with little guidance, and is starting to sound out words. Furthermore, David not only counts to 20, usually without mistakes, but also suggests using counting to figure out the answer to questions, such as "How do we know that more students voted for apples as their favorite fruit?"

Like all of the students in my class, David came to me in September with certain strengths and with plenty of room to grow, both socially and academically. I responded to these complexities with a multifaceted approach that reflects and addresses the needs of the whole child. His progress highlights the ways pre-K can positively affect several developmental areas as well as the important, collaborative role that parents can play in building a strong foundation for their children.

MAY 7

Becoming Social: Karen's Journey into Our Community

Karen's grandmother told me from day one that she was concerned about her granddaughter's social skills. Karen had never been to school before, and spent most of her time around adults: uncles, grandparents, and cousins. Karen already excelled in basic literacy and math skills after working one-on-one with her great grandmother, a retired schoolteacher, for the past year. Her transformation into a highly sociable member of our classroom community highlights the benefits of pre-K, even for those children who can attain academic readiness at home.

Karen's strengths and experiences led her to focus on reading, writing, and interacting with Ms. Morrison and me in the fall. She chose to read in the Library, play with table toys, or paint by herself during center time. Like David, she was quite hesitant to join her fellow four-year-olds in more social centers, such as the Dramatic Play and Blocks Centers. Yet she listened to and comprehended stories we read on the rug, could write her name, and was starting to make connections between letters and their sounds. While I kept challenging her with her academics, I knew the real challenge for Karen would be getting her to develop relationships with her peers.

I exposed Karen to the same community-building lessons as I did David. Unfortunately, group songs about our friends and role-playing with puppets did not motivate Karen to socialize with her friends. She would cheer on her friends and participate in role-plays at the rug, but then continue to play on her own during time. I needed to use a more proactive, involved approach that both reflected Karen's current comfort level and built on that comfort level to further her social development.

Karen gravitated toward me and listened to me because I was an adult. With that in mind, I invited Karen to play with me, and then suggested we either join her peers or invite them to play with us. She agreed, and over time, discovered how much fun her friends could be! I remember her laughing with Samar in the Discovery Center while they tested magnets with various materials. This December, she had even started problem solving independently with her friends.

Karen has come a long way since September. Just this week, she chose to go to the Dramatic Play Center, and I observed her taking her friends' orders in our pretend restaurant. She and her friends joked about changing their names in the Sand Center last month. She still sometimes prefers "alone time," such as the time she became adamant about separating the seal from the alligator in the Water Center so the seal would be safe. Yet she frequently experienced the very social interactions that will help her build and nurture relationships for years to come.

MAY 10

Center Time=Critical Time for Student Growth

"Center Time" is a critical time for pre-K students. It is here, especially, that they grow academically and socially. During center time in my classroom, the children can go to any of 10 interest areas that provide a wide range of opportunities for learning through hands-on, experiential activities. Each area has labeled materials and books pertinent to that area (for example, the Blocks Center has books about building and transportation, the Dramatic Play Center has cooking and career books, and the Art Center has art books full of famous paintings). These materials help teach how literacy permeates all areas of life.

Here is a glimpse into choice time in Pre-K 114:

- Blocks—The Blocks Center contains different types of blocks—wooden and plastic, large and small. In addition, we have worker hats, transportation toys, animal toys, and people figurines. We put illustrated labels on all toys to help the students become aware of letters and words, as well as how to use print in a functional way. I recall David and Samar once trying to construct a tunnel through which a toy car could pass. I asked them to remember what the tunnel looked like in a book we had recently read. They found the book and discovered they were missing the top part of the tunnel. They also learned about cause and effect when they pushed a car through their construction project too fast and its tall sides fell in.

- Dramatic Play—This center includes everything from plastic fruit to a medical kit. The children take on pretend roles, from mommies and daddies to doctors and waiters. We expose the students to the various functions of print by including real maps, menus, recipe books, and bus schedules to support their play. I often engage students by asking open-ended questions that build their vocabulary and target their individual needs. In the "doctor's office," I recently asked Doctor Tyrique whether he was going to fill out a prescription for my medicine. He responded by grabbing a notepad and writing my name. We worked on listening for the sounds in *Pappas* and connecting those sounds to letters.

- Art—This center includes a wide range of materials intended to spark the children's creativity and invite constructive and open-ended exploration. Rather than tell children exactly what to make, we give them tools such as watercolor paint, paint markers, hard and soft clay, and collage materials. Then we provide a sample piece for the children to look at and encourage the children to express themselves with their tools. For example, I once showed students how to paint on one side of a piece of paper, and then make a mirror image on the other side by folding the paper in half. The children then made their own paintings and, in the process, learned about symmetry.

These examples reveal the successful results of learning through play (what I like to call "constructive" play)—creating interest areas with opportunities for students to explore and grow in various content areas. Then I can use choice time as a way to target individual student needs identified through ongoing, performance-based assessments and analysis. As students explore and discover, I can use these teachable moments to move my students forward.

JUNE 7

The Pudding

The results are in! After nine months of instructing and assessing in various forms, I have comprehensive data on my students' growth in literacy. How did they do? Each child achieved an average of 80% or better on a wide range of literacy assessments!

Because pre-K students often do not show you everything they know or can do with one type of assessment, I used two types of assessments, and incorporated all the objectives from each into my calculations. I used a performance-based assessment that included anecdotes and work samples collected while the children played and interacted throughout the day, and supplemented these assessments with standardized assessments administered by me to each child. These standardized assessments tested skills such as letter identification and awareness of rhyming words.

Overall, 10 children out of the 14 children achieved 100% on the standardized assessments, and 9 achieved 90% or higher on the performance-based assessments. I am especially impressed by the individual gains made by the children, such as:

- Awana, who often struggled to move forward in letter identification and listening skills, in the end scored 85% on the standardized assessments and 83% on the performance-based assessments.
- Tanasia, who started the year too shy even to come to school the first day, scored 100% mastery on the standardized assessments and 88% on the performance-based assessments.

I realize that some in the early childhood community are skeptical about the extent to which standardized assessments are developmentally appropriate. I agree that such tests could potentially produce inaccurate results, given the young age of my students. I try to reduce the potential for inaccuracies by identifying the assessments as "fun games to play with the teacher," which can help the children feel more at ease and less stressed by the experience. I ask students if they would like to play with me, and many times they jump at the chance to spend some one-on-one time with me, especially because they get to press the "easy" button (thanks, Staples) when they finish. I remember Tyrique was sad that he could not play our "game" a second time.

Consistency between the scores given by the two types of assessments suggests that these techniques can help produce more reliable results than the results culled from a strictly standardized assessment. The results also show general consistency between the two kinds of assessments.

Standardized assessments are necessary in my case because the kindergarten teachers who will have my students next year use standardized assessments and not performance-based assessments. Of course, this begs the question: Why don't kindergarten teachers use performance-based assessments? I think kindergarten teachers should use some combination of the two, at a minimum, to gain a more comprehensive understanding of their students' strengths and needs.

I am very proud of my students' growth and know that my efforts, combined with the efforts of Ms. Morrison, Ms. Mills, and each child's family, contributed to the students' success.

Families, Students, and School—Building a Strong Foundation

Introduction

During my three years in the classroom, I viewed my students' families as their first teacher and the most direct stakeholder in their lives. At the end of the school year, I would send the children off to kindergarten, and they would have over a dozen other schoolteachers after me. Yet their families would retain a constant presence throughout their lives. Our partnership was therefore crucial to their children's success in the long run. I established an open and welcoming environment that belonged to all of us, communicated frequently with families, and identified various ways they could be involved. The two formal parent-teacher conferences would not suffice nor would a rigid menu of options for familial involvement. Some family members who worked in the afternoon and evenings could volunteer to read to us in the morning, whereas others opted to send in snack periodically because they worked during the day and communicate with me regularly with weekly notes. We all want what is best for kids, and when I built off of the love and the goals family members already had for their children, I was able to establish trust and cooperation.

DECEMBER 10

Learning from Each Other

Partnership and cooperation between teachers and families are so critical to children's success in pre-K. What happens at home impacts events at school, and vice versa. Even though I spend months interacting with my students, recording their progress, and collecting their work samples, I need family involvement to help me fully understand each child's interests and needs. And I need families' trust if I am going to get the information, information that—as David's mother put it—will help these children "go sky high and have a better life."

For example, last week our school held a parent-teacher conference night. Well before that week, I laid the groundwork to make sure my students' families came. I shared information about their children's progress 2–3 times per week, either orally for those family members who drop off and pick up their children, or through informal notes to those family members who work during school hours. I also reinforced that family members are always welcome in my classroom. One way I do this is by inviting families to special events, like "Family Show and Tell" and our "Giving Thanks Party." The use of both formal, written invitations and constant oral reminders to families helps boost attendance and demonstrates my sincere desire to make each family member a part of their child's education. During conferences, I prefer to use an open dialogue format. I find it more effective than a format in which I do all the talking. Rather than just delivering and explaining a child's report card, I use an individualized action plan (see sample on page 185) to guide the discussion of the child's strengths, target areas, and the ways that both the student's family and I can help the student continue to develop and grow.

This last time, 13 out of 14 parents or guardians showed up for conferences. Several of these family members remarked that their children do things like rhyming and retelling stories at home—often these are the activities that these same children did not participate in while they were in the classroom! This information is invaluable; it illustrates how a child's reluctance to participate in certain activities does not necessarily indicate inability, but simply a lack of comfort in the classroom. With this information in mind, I can design teaching strategies that more accurately reflect each child's needs. Thank you, families! Results like these prove that families will make time to be involved if teachers make time for them and create strong connections between the home and school.

JANUARY 9

A New Year: Pre-K 114's Resolutions for 2007

In my classroom, setting goals and working tirelessly to achieve them is a crucial part of our overarching theme of going from "good to great." I set goals for my students, use data to assess their progress toward those goals, and design lessons based on those analyses. Likewise, I aim to instill in my students an understanding of the importance of reflecting about areas in which they can improve, and then addressing those areas to help them grow as learners. I also want to families to feel invested in this process, in order to ensure that my students continue to live and think with goal-oriented mindsets even after they graduate from pre-K.

As part of our celebration of the New Year, we made resolutions with our families. Each student received a note and a blank resolution card the first day back last week. Students returned the cards after coming up with resolutions while at home with their families. Here are several examples:

Tyrone and his mother:

Our goal is to read more words and count more numbers.

David and his mother:

Our goal is to read two books every night, and learn more words and letters.

Sierra and her family:

As a family, our goal is to spend more time reading and sharing our thoughts.

Derrell and his mother:

Our goal is to improve Derrell's writing of letters.

Tyrique and his mother:

Our goal is to strive for the best together.

Awana and her mother:

Our goal is to identify numbers and the letters and to work on writing Awana's first and last name.

Karen and her grandmother:

Our goal is to read one new book a night and write down two new words out of the book.

Fuquan and his mother:

Our goal is to read a book every night.

Kevin and his grandmother:

Our goal is to help Kevin read a book until he understands how to read alone.

Jeffrey and his mother:

Our goal is to learn how to tie our shoelaces.

Ravon, his mother and father:

Our goal is to sing more songs together, such as "The Wheels on the Bus."

JANUARY 21

And Still He Rises...

Friday morning, 7:45a.m., and still no Ms. Alexander. Tyrique's mother and I have now set up four alternative conference times to meet about Tyrique. Each time she has said she would make it. Each time I have provided several oral and written reminders, and each time, she has not shown. Tyrique is not a major behavior problem in the classroom, but he is developing academically more slowly than the other students in the class. He could barely identify any of the letters in his name and struggled to develop basic book-handling skills when he first came into the classroom back in September. Ms. Alexander and I have a lot to discuss, but still she has not come. She does come, however, to other family events: Family Show-and-Tell, Giving Thanks, Halloween Costume Parade, Tyrique's birthday party. Even for these events, she comes late, but she does come, nonetheless.

Frustrated by Ms. Alexander's frequent no-shows, I decide to focus more on Tyrique and our work inside the classroom. With our efforts to target his needs in one-on-one, small group, and whole group interactions, Tyrique has now started on his own to identify beginning sounds and more letters in words. He can also write his name and read the names of his friends.

Is family support important? Of course. But what happens when difficulties with familial investment arise, even as early as pre-K? Does the child become a lost cause? Of course not. Should teachers relinquish their own responsibility? Just the opposite.

JANUARY 23

Home-School Disconnection

From encouraging high attendance at special events to creating an open and inviting dialogue at one-on-one conferences, my relationships with students' families this year have been both positive and strong. That is until last Thursday.

Early one morning, as I welcomed Kevin and his grandmother with my usual energetic greeting during the before-school program, Kevin's grandmother abruptly cut me off with sharp and heated criticism of the homework assignments I had sent home. She wanted to know when I would be sending home "letter work," like she has seen in "all the daycare centers." She said she was bothered by all the open-ended assignments I was giving Kevin. These assignments often include searching for letters around the house, looking on food containers and in magazines, or having Kevin use his own drawings to tell a story, and then dictate the story to an adult.

Kevin's grandmother's bottom line was this: She wanted dittos. There, I said it, the "d" word, dreaded among early childhood experts.

Like them, I advocate a different "d" approach, one that is perhaps the antithesis of the malignant ditto: "Developmentally Appropriate Practices." After saying that she wanted her grandson using dittos, Kevin's grandmother then went on to critique my methods of teaching of during the day, arguing that I wasn't "teaching Kevin his letters" and that she would instead have "to buy some workbooks for him to use at home."

As a pre-K teacher striving to meet my class's developmental needs, I provide my students with plenty of opportunities to learn through hands-on experiences that are meaningful to them. If the Sand and Water Table interests Kevin, he will find plenty of letter tools with which to explore the alphabet. If he chooses to pretend he is a doctor in the Dramatic Play Center, Kevin will surely learn about letters and, equally as important, why we use them as he writes down his patients' diagnoses and prescriptions. I also supplement this experiential learning with various letter songs and games.

I could not help but wonder how pages of letter matching and tracing activities would help build a strong foundation in early literacy for Kevin. To top it off, Kevin actually knows all of his letters and the letter sounds. We are currently working on sounding out letter sounds and writing words. When I tried to explain my strategies and Kevin's progress, she just replied, "I don't want to hear it. I know all about learning through play. I don't want to hear it." She then proceeded to storm out, leaving me feeling puzzled, challenged professionally, and, quite frankly, nauseous.

It is now January. I have had one formal one-on-one conference with Kevin's grandmother, as well as several informal conversations at our special events. She has never once mentioned any concern about our work. I am not sure what exactly prompted the negative exchange, but I do know that it hurt our relationship. I suppose I could treat her comments as an irrational rant, and just keep doing what I am doing. However, as a teacher, I serve my students and their families. If there is a conflict, I feel that it is my responsibility as the classroom leader to think objectively about how best to handle the situation.

I have decided to provide Kevin's grandmother and the rest of my students' families with a list of ways we teach letters and letter sounds in the classroom. I look forward to hearing her response.

FEBRUARY 26

Lessons in Diplomacy

Last week, I had another round of bilateral talks—a.k.a. parent-teacher conferences—which again revealed the importance for pre-K teachers to possess good "diplomatic skills."

Going into the conferences, I felt enthusiastic about discussing my students' progress. Tanasia, who had struggled to come out of her shell, is now participating throughout the day and moving forward in basic math and literacy skills. A look at David's writing folder demonstrates clear and constant growth, progressing from self-portraits he labeled with the letter "D" to short sentences written with little guidance using invented spelling.

I grew concerned, though, as I considered a few remaining difficulties with two family members in particular: Kevin's grandmother, who emphatically disapproves of our literacy program; and Tyrique's mother, who, after more than five attempts to reschedule during the last cycle of conferences, still has not made it to a scheduled conference.

Despite my efforts to engage her, Kevin's grandmother barely spoke to me since our confrontation in January. She did, however, continue to complain to Ms. Morrison during the after-school program, proclaiming, "I can't wait until this year is over." While this round of conferences was supposed to focus more heavily on social development and the explanation of a new assessment strategy, I decided to start my conversation with Kevin's grandmother with some positive comments relating to her primary concern: literacy. I began by discussing Kevin's ability to read short sentences with little guidance from me (for example, he can read, "I like to see the fat cat run on the mat."). I showed her a short, teacher-made assessment I gave to Kevin the day before and modeled how he used his knowledge of letters, letter sounds, and sight words to read. She was so overjoyed with this positive communication that I was able to shift gears and discuss Kevin's need for further development in other skill areas, such as taking on roles in dramatic play, taking turns, and using words to solve conflicts. After the meeting, I felt overjoyed to see Kevin's grandmother recognizing the progress Kevin made developing his literacy skills through the activities and lesson I prepared.

Given her absence from the previous conference, I did not expect Tyrique's mother to respond to the school's formal efforts to set up conferences for this round. I, therefore, made plans to reach out to her informally about two weeks before. In addition to mentioning something positive about Tyrique's performance each time she came in, I would say that I looked forward to talking more about Tyrique and to use the conference time to show his mother what great work he has done. The day of the conferences, Tyrique's mother said she couldn't stay, but we rescheduled for the next morning. I made a comment about meeting to discuss Tyrique over muffins in the morning. She laughed, and at 7:45 the next morning, Tyrique's mother was at my door. We had a productive conference and even discussed some behavioral issues, issues that she said she had noticed at home as well.

In both of these cases, I believe it was my ability to talk with family members about their children in a positive light that helped us get past their initial indifference and hostility. It goes to show that, even when teachers and family members do not see eye to eye or see each other frequently, communication between a child's home and school is achievable and beneficial to all.

MARCH 16

Women Making History in Our Own Lives

As a pre-K teacher in a school-based setting, I needed to think critically about how to incorporate school-wide celebrations and events into our classroom in an age-appropriate way. We began our exploration of Black History Month by celebrating ourselves and the diversity of others using a book donated by Tyrone's mother, *Shades of Black* by Sandra Pinkney. After reading and discussing the book, we did a role-play of Rosa Parks on the bus, and sang a song about Dr. Martin Luther King, Jr. For election day, we discussed and voted on our favorite center using a secret ballot.

Women's History Month was a bit trickier until I applied a general rule used in the other examples: How can we celebrate this event in a way that is meaningful to the children and lays the foundation for a more nuanced understanding of the event in the future?

I decided to focus on women playing an important role in their lives. We first made a web diagram of different types of women in our lives (for example, mother, sister, cousin, aunt, grandmother, family friend, and so on). We then discussed the significant contributions of these women and planned an event to celebrate them. We created an invitation and letter to the women using interactive writing, and each child wrote their own story about their experience with the women in their lives.

I had observed the investment of many of these women in their children's education throughout the year and also saw firsthand how special the women in our larger community are. Here are just a few examples:
- Two elderly women with grandchildren at my school frequently sat on their front stoop or stood on the bus corner while I waited for the 70 to take me downtown. They inquired about my day and conversed with me about local politics and the history of the neighborhood:
- The female crossing guard and Awana's aunt would tell the bus to wait if they saw me coming and motion to me to start running from down the block.
- Awana's mother, even before Awana was my student, would watch me from her bedroom window while she read to make sure I was safe on the corner.

In the end, the celebration thrilled the family members and friends who attended, gave a sense of pride to the students who prepared the food and writing, and reaffirmed my belief that I share with my students' families the belief in doing what is best for the children.

APRIL 6

The Benefits of Pre-K: A Family Member's Perspective

After reading reports about the link between childcare and children's negative behavior in future years, I thought it might be helpful to hear a family member's take on the effect pre-K was having on her son's development. I decided to interview Ravon's mother. I asked her, "Why did you decide to enroll Ravon in pre-K?"

"I did not want a lot of play for Ravon. My younger brother was in your class the previous year, and I always liked the way you involved the families in the homework assignments. I like the interaction with Ravon and me because I know what he is learning and we can work on further developing his listening and language skills together. In addition, though you still let the children play in your classroom, they learn through that play. Daycare was just play, play, color, color, all day long; there was not enough learning."

"What do you think about the recent studies that link childcare programs with negative behavior later on?"

"Well, I used to work in daycare, so I agree. Daycare programs tend to "baby" the children instead of giving the children ways to solve problems when they misbehave. They do not explain things as much. The regular elementary-school pre-K is different. You explain to the child why they are wrong and how they can correct themselves."

"How much education do you think a pre-K teacher needs in order to benefit children?"

"I think experience goes a long way, often more than education. Some people with more experience than education can deal with children better. My grandmother had no education and kept eight children in line."

"What are the benefits of pre-K?"

"I have seen so much growth with Ravon. He is expressing himself better. He is more disciplined, and he wants to come to school. He does not want to miss a day. My husband and I are so happy."

"What are your hopes for Ravon?"

"My hopes are that Ravon can write, express himself more clearly, interpret things better, and read at least on his level."

"What about in the long run?"

"I want my son to go to college. I want him to have a very decent job. I want him to enjoy what he does. It is not as much about the money. I really want him to be happy."

When this entry first appeared on the Pre-K Now blog, Kathleen O'Pray responded with comments on her experience with strong and weak pre-K programs:

> I share your concern for providing quality childcare. I have worked in early childhood for a number of years and have seen the positive development children can show when they are in a quality program. I have also seen the results of programs that are not based on long-term planning and knowledge of childhood development. The difference is often the training and education of the teachers knowing the long-term results of the actions taken in the classroom.

JUNE 19

Summer Learning

The retention of skills and knowledge from one school year to the next is crucial for students of any age, including students transitioning from pre-K to kindergarten. Because my program is a school year, not one that runs throughout the year, I make extra effort to get my class's families committed to summertime learning.

I've seen first-hand what can happen when that effort and commitment are lacking. After my first year of teaching, I ran into a former student and her mother on the bus, right before the new school year began. In our conversation, I discovered that the child had regressed both academically and socially. Subsequent discussions with some of my school's kindergarten teachers revealed that this child's experience was not unique.

Once I moved past the initial frustration and disappointment, I began thinking about how best to ensure that the learning foundation established in my classroom did not crumble after Pre-K Graduation Day. My first thought was to recommend to families some summer programs for young children. It turns out, my district does not offer such programs for pre-Kindergartners, and affordable non-school-based options are scarce.

Next, I decided to create summer-learning supports for the families. In the past, I had sent home books and writing materials for the summer, but had not strategically designed tools to meet my students' needs. Sure, I gave families their child's assessment results and general tips for keeping their children engaged over the summer, but this proved insufficient as it meant more work for busy families, forcing them to choose and create learning activities based on this information. Now, I give families a homework packet with specific activities they can do with their children and the materials needed to do them. There are no dittos in the packet; instead, there are various opportunities for the children to review and continue to explore letters, words, writing, numbers, and shapes.

Judging by my class's high return rate for homework packets distributed at other school-year breaks (over 85%!), I am confident that my students' families will work with their children on these activities during the summer. Because of this family involvement, I am hopeful that my students' school readiness in the fall will be equal to or even greater than it was on their last day of pre-K.

Epilogue

On June 27, 2007, I left pre-K 114 for the last time. My students went on to kindergarten and left me with love, pride, and questions. Their stories challenge the misconception that circumstances at home prevent success at school. I saw Tanasia go from not knowing what a letter was to writing basic sentences. I heard Tyrique sound out a word and exclaim, "I'm a great reader, Ms. Pappas!" in May after coming to school in the fall unable to sit still or hold a book correctly. Thinking about these and other success stories, I wondered what the experiences of other children were like before entering kindergarten, and what would happen to my kids in subsequent grades, as well as in life in general. I could not say that every child in our country would have fully enriching, productive, and healthy lives. I could, however, envision a time when this *becomes* our reality. I could criticize existing policies and begin to consider how to improve them based on the lessons I learned from my students, their families, Ms. Morrison, the rest of my school community, and Teach For America. I felt torn, that day, between continuing to have a direct impact on children as a teacher and taking my insights and energy and redirecting them toward larger policy issues.

At that same time, Teach For America was finishing the first year of its strategic initiative to bring some of our nation's most promising future leaders into pre-K classrooms. I decided to join the staff and help spearhead the development of a sustainable Teach For America early childhood presence in more urban and rural areas across the country. We managed to increase the number of Teach For America regions with pre-K from six to 11, and lay the foundation to ensure that we can continue to place and support hundreds of corps members in pre-K classrooms. In the end, these teachers will have a catalytic effect on broader efforts to reform early childhood education. They will become excellent teachers, school leaders, policymakers, and advocates for change in other related sectors. During that year, I also learned about the pre-K policies in 14 states and had the privilege to gain insight into the nuances of early childhood education policy from experts in the field. Lastly, I was able to stay in communication with my former students, most of who stayed at Carter and were now in Ms. Grigg's kindergarten class. She was happy to report that they were all on or above grade level. We corresponded through letters, and I visited the classroom several times. I was ecstatic to see my former students reading, writing, and continuing to think critically about stories. Samar argued that the fox in *Henny Penny* probably dropped the acorn at the beginning of the story as a way to lure the animals into his den. Tanasia was excited to show me how she was sounding out words and was persistent even with the challenging ones. David proudly shared the news that his mother is now a nurse, and he helped his friends read on the carpet using our shoulder-elbow-wrist strategy. Unfortunately, I did not get to see those students who moved away, but I hope they are doing well and that I have the privilege of getting in touch with them in the future.

One of the first lessons I learned as a college undergraduate was about the power that comes from being able to set agendas in any context. I could give my students a voice in a variety of ways, including this book and the blog I wrote. However, giving voice to their needs does not effectively help reset the education agenda in the United States. My students and all young children also need elected officials who understand policy and who represent their interests when identifying major priorities and making tough decisions. My experiences at Teach For America, while immensely rewarding in and of themselves, made me want to situate my understanding of pre-K within broader political and economic frameworks, and invest a broad base of citizens in my vision for change. My students' growth and the development of my partnership with their families taught me the importance of staying in tune with your community. The countless hours I spent taking and analyzing anecdotal notes about my students and learning from Mark (my Teach For America program director), Ms. Morrison, and other teachers helped equip me with the tools I needed to meet my students' needs. To do that on a larger scale and in a more comprehensive way, I need to learn more about policy, politics, and government. To do that, I am pursuing a Master in Public Policy at the Kennedy School of Government.

On June 27, 2007, I may have left my classroom, but from that classroom I brought with me the interests, challenges, and successes of my students. These memories traveled from Newark, New Jersey to Cambridge, Massachusetts in the form of work samples, the yearbooks we made each year, and a Tinker Bell Santa watch one of my students gave me my second year in the classroom. These objects are a daily reminder of why I am here and what I aim to accomplish. They connect me to the need for sustained and coordinated leadership focused on eliminating educational inequity and the proof that we can ensure all children have equal chances in life.

Afterword

Wendy Kopp, the founder and president of Teach For America, based her theory of change on the belief that after spending at least two years in a low-income urban or rural classroom, individuals like me would, for the rest of our lives, have the conviction and insight needed to drive our efforts to eliminate educational inequities. I understood that concept on an intellectual level when I entered the corps, but grasped its full implications only as I promoted my final class of pre-K students to kindergarten.

Before I entered the classroom as a corps member, my academic exploration of race and class as an undergraduate at Georgetown made me angry at the injustices in our society. Each day I spent as a teacher was another chance for me to provide my students with the foundational skills and high expectations they need to achieve. After teaching for three years, it frightens me to think that something external or systemic may be holding my students back from realizing their potential.

Common perceptions of race and educational equity within a historical and contemporary perspective reveal key differences between conventional wisdom and my experiences. The key challenge to my students' ability to realize their potential is not necessarily someone demeaning them by saying, "You can't go to college or pursue the career of your choice because you're black." The overt racism that once plagued our nation may be in significant decline, but for many young African Americans and other minorities a number of other institutional failings still adversely affect the scope of their life prospects. Take, for instance, the teacher who fails to make school an exciting and welcoming place in which all children can grow as learners and members of a community. Take the principal who neglects to lead a school with a vision of excellence. Take the school district that enables the stagnant and entrenched interests of particular groups to prevent both the cultivation of talent and the removal of weak educators. Take the state and federal agencies that provide money and benchmarks but not incentives for sustained and coordinated leadership. In the end, it is the failings of these individuals and organizations that hold our society back from fulfilling its promise of providing equity and justice for all.

That said, the excess of attention paid to ineffective teachers and administrators disturbs me. As a beginning teacher, I learned a great deal from other teachers deeply committed to the growth of students. The negative stories drown out the successes of strong teachers.

This happens because high-quality educators (including the second grade teacher at my school whose students wrote incredibly creative and engaging pieces of writing, as well as the many teachers who came to school early and stayed late to tutor children) are too busy focusing on their students' achievement to spend time countering the complaints of their more negative colleagues.

Teachers are not solely to blame. The system often encourages teachers to focus on providing only a minimum level of commitment. This is evident, for instance, in the peculiar obsession some teachers have with the time they spend away from the students, the very people whom they are supposed to serve. At the first orientation I attended for the School Leadership Team in my district, one of the administrators set the bar quite low when he said, "Six-and-a-half hours—all we ask is that you give all you have for six-and-a-half hours per day, ten months a year." True, he was asking us to invest energy into our classrooms, but if I "gave all I had" for only those six-and-a-half hours a day, ten months a year, I never would have succeeded with my students. The hours I spent preparing before and after school, on the weekends, and in the summer, proved crucial to helping my students grow and learn. At one of my first professional-development workshops, I thought that the facilitator undermined her entire presentation by ending the session with this "comforting" remark:

"And if these strategies don't work, just keep this in mind, that in a few weeks we have Columbus Day, and a few weeks after that is Veteran's Day." She then proceeded to name each holiday from September to June. The thorough nature of this closing statement—in fact more thorough than any other part of her session—validated and perpetuated a perspective on education that puts the teachers' schedules first and students' needs second.

As someone who, as my father says, has never shied away from expressing her opinion, I realize that, to some, my points may come across as naïve, and even unfair. I will certainly learn more about the nuances of our education system as a graduate student in public policy and, hopefully, from working with public servants. I hope that these experiences will help me become a stronger, smarter, more effective leader. I also know that the gap in achievement is a problem that we in the educational community can solve. I know this from teaching my students, from observing the common educational practices at my school and district, and from visiting classrooms and schools across the country where committed teachers and administrators successfully help their students learn and succeed. While there are some individuals perpetuating inequities, there are still more beating the odds every day: the veteran teacher in Chicago who skillfully uses her years of experience to raise the bar for her students; the second-year Teach For America corps member in Houston working relentlessly to bring her students up to the national standard for their age; the first-year school leader in Camden determined to turn his school around by using an alternative model that utilizes longer school days, family contracts, and aggressive teacher-recruitment strategies; or the mayor who dares to hold himself accountable. The deficiencies in our system are tragic and antithetical to the very principles that make our country great. But they can be rectified if we—voters, policymakers, journalists, non-profit organizations, educators, family members—recognize our roles as stakeholders in the lives of the students, and as people who can work together to foster positive systemic change.

Appendix

Sample Individual Action Plan

Student's name: Kevin
Date: November 30, 2006

Pre-K 114, Ms. Pappas
General Summary

Strengths

- Following two step directions; listening during circle time
- Identifying his name and the names of his friends
- Starting to identify more letters, especially those in his name
- Starting to make some letter-sound connections; playing with words more
- Using sentences with 5–6 words; asking questions
- Listening to and comprehending stories

Target Areas

- Incorporating ideas from discussions, books, and activities into play (during center time)
- Repeating parts of stories and songs

- Using role appropriate language (for instance, "I'm the daddy") during play
- Using vocabulary from stories and discussions in play time
- Developing letter and word identification
- Recognizing classroom print (words, not pictures)
- Using print for different functions (labeling, grocery list, and so on)
- Relating stories to his own life; asking questions about stories
- Rhyming and playing with letter sounds on his own
- Writing letters and words as part of play

What I plan to do:

- Discuss with **Kevin** before center time how he might use ideas from discussions in play (planning, for example, how he might build a restaurant from a story in blocks).
- Engage **Kevin** in role discussions when he is in the play areas.
- Think aloud more, connecting stories to my life; encourage **Kevin** to do the same.
- Develop more one-on-one and small-group letter explorations (games link B-I-N-G-O, concentration, and letter hunts); writing/creating letters with different materials (such as shaving cream, playdough, string, and so on).

- Work one-on-one to help the child write his name during sign-in time more frequently, and help him with writing letters and words.
- Rhyme with him during play time.

What you (student's family member[s]) can do:

- Go on a print and letter hunt at home—look for print and letters in magazines, newspapers, and so on.
- Invite **Kevin** to write with you (grocery list, taking a phone message, writing a letter, and so on).
- Encourage him to practice the sight words we learn at home and to label pictures he draws.
    (**Note:** You may want to give him a journal in which he can write words, draw pictures, and label the pictures.)
- Ask him comprehension and critical thinking questions when you read to him (for instance, "what would you have done differently?" or "What do you think happens after the story is over/before it began?")

Individual Action Plan

Student's name:
Date:

General Summary

Strengths

_____
_____
_____
_____

Target Areas

_____
_____
_____
_____

What I plan to do:

_____
_____
_____
_____

What you (student's family member[s]) can do:

_____
_____
_____
_____

The publisher grants permission for this page to be photocopied for distribution for teachers' classroom use only. © Gryphon House, Inc. www.gryphonhouse.com

General process a teacher can follow to create individualized behavior contracts:

1. Verify that the whole-class consequence system is not working.
2. Talk to the student's parent or family member first before creating the contract to discuss the strategies you have already tried, what the parent or family member has tried at home, and the possibility of using a contract.
3. Try additional strategies introduced by the parent or family member.
4. Use the template below as a guide in your conversation with the student, but make sure to frame it as a casual conversation with the student.
5. Come to the conversation prepared with a clear sense of the specific behaviors you are trying to change. If there are multiple behaviors, I would suggest starting with one (for example, listening quietly while teachers or students are talking).
6. Set aside some time to discuss the contract when the child will not be distracted (for example, I sat down with Ali in between breakfast and circle time as opposed to

center time when I knew she would be significantly more engaged in an activity)
7. Make sure to have a sense of what the child might identify as an appealing incentive. Children may not be used to contributing to this type of process, so you may need to use the child's interest as a starting point.
8. Figure out a point system that meets the child where he or she is with their math skills. The child may not be ready for a system like the one described below, which adds up points over time. You may need to do something on a daily basis.
9. Set up a system to report and discuss the results of the contract with the student's family (through phone calls and in-person meetings), depending on the family member's schedule.

Individualized Behavior Contract

I, _____, hereby agree to_____
_____
_____

This job will be a success if I receive 15 or more points for the week.

For the successful completion of this job I will get to

_____
_____
_____
_____
_____

I, _____, will assess _____'s behavior on a scale from 1–4 (4 being the most well behaved) each day. I will mark _____'s score in the boxes below and send the contract back to _____ on Friday.

Monday	Tuesday	Wednesday	Thursday	Friday

Student Signature: _____

Teacher Signature: _____

Parent/Guardian Signature: _____

Date: _____

The publisher grants permission for this page to be photocopied for distribution for teachers' classroom use only. © Gryphon House, Inc. www.gryphonhouse.com

Family Library

All Are Welcome!

As part of my overall plan to get the students excited about reading, I am creating a family library in the classroom. On a daily basis, you and your child can take out books from this library. Below you will find a blank family library card for you and your child. Please fill out the card and return the bottom half of this sheet to me in this folder as soon as possible so that I can laminate your card.

Over time, I hope to develop a Family Picks section in our classroom library that will consist of books that are highly recommended by students' families.

Together, we can generate enthusiasm for books and let the children experience a wide variety of stories.

FAMILY LIBRARY CARD

Issued by _____ to

_____ and
(parent/guardian's name)

_____
(student's name)

so that they may enjoy our classroom library at home together!

The publisher grants permission for this page to be photocopied for distribution for teachers' classroom use only. © Gryphon House, Inc. www.gryphonhouse.com

Back Cover Material

Based on the author's pop Pre-K Now blog, Good Morning, Children provides a personal view of the challenges and of a beginning teacher. The book describes daily encounters with students, family members, and administrators; reflects on the state of early childhood education in America; and celebrates the ways pre-K teachers can help prepare every child to succeed in both school and life.

Sophia E. Pappas was a model teacher for both novice and veteran pre-K educators in Newark, New Jersey and Teach For America teachers in rural and urban regions across the country. She also led Teach For America's effort to expand its presence in early childhood education programs nationwide. Sophia is currently pursuing a Master in Public Policy degree at Harvard University, where she is a participant in the program, From Harvard Square to the Oval office. She lives in Cambridge, Massachusetts.

"This book brings the voices of a Teach For America teacher and her students into the public discussion about how to provide children with the early education necessary to set them up for long-term success. Sophia chronicles her accomplishments and challenges in ensuring that her economically disadvantaged students can excel, and she communicates important insights about how to (give) all of our nation's children the educational opportunities they deserve."

>—Wendy Kopp, Chief Executive Officer and Founder of Teach For America

"...(This book) provides vital lessons for any teacher and for all those involved in designing policies and programs to promote the success of early childhood educators and their young pupils.... The candid voice that reveals (Ms. Pappas') missteps and accomplishments (offers) a unique combination of persistence, vision, and humility."

>—Libby Doggett, Deputy Director, Pew Center on the States

"...Sophia's hunger for educational equity—borne out of the obstacles and triumphs she experienced in the classroom—makes her an exciting leader and change agent to watch...."

>—Daniel R. Porterfield, Ph.D., Senior Vice President for Strategic Development, Georgetown University

Books For ALL Kinds of Readers

At ReadHowYouWant we understand that one size does not fit all types of readers. Our innovative, patent pending technology allows us to design new formats to make reading easier and more enjoyable for you. This helps improve your speed of reading and your comprehension. Our EasyRead printed books have been optimized to improve word recognition, ease eye tracking by adjusting word and line spacing as well as minimizing hyphenation. Our EasyRead SuperLarge editions have been developed to make reading easier and more accessible for vision-impaired readers. We offer Braille and DAISY formats of our books and all popular E-Book formats.

We are continually introducing new formats based upon research and reader preferences. Visit our web-site to see all of our formats and learn how you can Personalize our books for yourself or as gifts. Sign up to Become A (RHYW) Registered Reader.

www.readhowyouwant.com